GREEN GUIDE No 13

Lecturing For Better Learning

Robert Cannon
and Christopher Knapper

Centre for Teaching and Learning
University of Windsor

STLHE SAPES

Society for Teaching and Learning in Higher Education
La société pour l'avancement de la pédagogie dans l'enseignement supérieur

This is a joint publication of HERSDA and STLHE

HERDSA Guide Series

Editor: Allan Goody, Curtin University

Committee: Barbara Grant, The University of Auckland

                        Roger Landbeck, HERDSA News Editor

                        Richard Ladyshewsky, Curtin University

                        Jo McKenzie, University of Technology Sydney

                        Kathryn Sutherland, Victoria University of Wellington

                        Gail Wilson, Southern Cross University

                        Ursula McGowan, The University of Adelaide

STLHE Green Guides

Series Editor: Dianne Bateman

                        Chair, STLHE Publications

                        Champlain Regional College

                        Saint Lambert Campus

Founding Series Editor: Christopher Knapper

Queen's University

Associate Series Editors: Roger Moore

                        Professor Emeritus

                        St. Thomas University

Publishing Coordinator: Sylvia Avery

                        STLHE Administrator

Director of Retail Services: Steve Alb

                        The Book Store at Western

                        The University of Western Ontario

Distributed on behalf of STLHE by: The Book Store at Western

                        University Community Centre

                        The University of Western Ontario

                        London, Ontario N6A 3K7

(STLHE Green Guide: 13)

Includes bibliographical references and index.

ISBN 978-0-9866132-3-4

Foreword

Dianne Bateman, PhD
Series Editor

We are proud to launch **Lecturing For Better Learning**, the thirteenth in STLHE's Green Guide Series. This Green Guide is special for many reasons. Its uniqueness can be found in its origins, authors and message.

The idea for the Green Guide series originated with our sister organization, the Higher Education and Research Development Society of Australasia (HERSDA). They have published Green Guides since 1984. Christopher Knapper, the Founding Series Editor for STLHE, introduced the idea to Canada in 1998 when he persuaded HERSDA to allow us to use their title for our own series. At that time HERSDA and STLHE agreed to collaborate on joint publications where appropriate. **Lecturing For Better Learning** is one of those appropriate occasions.

This third edition speaks to the continued collaboration of its authors, Bob Cannon and Christopher Knapper, the partnership between HERSDA and STLHE and to the continued interest in lecturing as one of the most popular methods of large group teaching.

With today's emphasis on active learning and smart classrooms, one might wonder why STLHE and HERSDA would publish a Green Guide on Lecturing. Bob and Chris acknowledge this contradiction but are quick to point out that given the popularity of lecturing, faculty and students are served when it is done well ; faculty are more satisfied and less stressed, while students learn more effectively. Their chapter, *Moving from Teacher Telling to Student learning in Lectures*, combined with their excellent list of recommended readings addresses this issue and simultaneously stresses the importance of achieving a balance in the instructional methods that we choose.

Green Guide #13 has something for both the novice and more experienced teacher. Both groups can benefit from the relevant research on which it is based, their pragmatic approach, and their deep understanding of the instructional challenges found in college and university classrooms.

In closing we would like to thank Bob and Chris for their continued collaboration and commitment to improving teaching and learning in higher education.

Introducing the Authors

ROBERT CANNON, MA HONOURS (SYDNEY), MED ADMIN, DIPTERTED (NEW ENGLAND)

Robert Cannon has been an active member of HERDSA since 1975 and was Associate Professor and Director of the Advisory Centre for University Education at The University of Adelaide. As Professor at the University of Indonesia between 1994 and 1997, he helped to establish Indonesia's first educational research and development centre. He has written widely on teaching and also on the development of education in Indonesia and is best known for his books written with David Newble – A Handbook for Teachers in Universities and Colleges (Kogan Page) and A Handbook for Medical Teachers (Kluwer).

CHRISTOPHER KNAPPER, BA (SHEFFIELD), PHD (SASKATCHEWAN)

Christopher Knapper is Professor Emeritus of Psychology and Director Emeritus of the Centre for Teaching and Learning at Queen's University, Canada. He was the first President of the Society for Teaching and Learning in Higher Education (STLHE) in Canada and founding editor of The International Journal for Academic Development. He has written widely on postsecondary teaching and learning and given workshops and courses in many parts of the world. Among his influential books is Lifelong Learning in Higher Education (Kogan Page) written with Arthur Cropley.

Contents

About this guide 10

About this third edition 11

How to use this guide 13

1. The effective lecturer 15

2. Lecture preparation 19

3. Lecture presentation 39

4. Evaluation of lectures 47

5. Moving from teacher telling to student learning in lectures 53

6. Recommended reading 63

References 65

About This Guide

Lecturing has been written with two audiences in mind. The primary audience is the beginning or inexperienced academic teacher looking for straightforward advice and ideas on ways to lecture to students. The second audience is a much larger one. This audience includes more experienced academics who may be seeking ideas on lecturing to achieve any one of a number of goals such as to improve lecturing as a learning method, or to make the task of lecturing a more personally rewarding and less stressful one.

The Guide retains the five-part structure of earlier editions:

- The Effective Lecturer provides a brief overview of the research associated with effective teaching in higher education. It is the basis for the following four sections.
- Lecture Preparation offers ideas for preparing both the content and the presentation of a lecture.
- Lecture Presentation describes the essentials of delivering a lecture.
- Lecture Evaluation deals with improving lectures through careful evaluation so that modifications or changes to practices can occur. This section describes a number of evaluative techniques to help in this important process.
- Moving from Teacher Telling to Student Learning in Lectures addresses concerns about the effectiveness of the traditional 50-minute lecture as a learning method. This final Chapter suggests general ways of using lecture time for more successful, challenging, and interesting ways of teaching large groups of students.

The Guide focuses on lecturing. It has been tempting, at times, to expand the discussion into other important and related issues such as assessment of student learning and alternative teaching methods. However, there is insufficient space in the Guide to do this well and there are other excellent Guides, numerous web resources, and books that do this quite comprehensively. Some of them are described in the text and others are listed Chapter 6, Recommended Reading.

About This Third Edition

This third edition has been prepared at the request of HERDSA as part of a program of updating the older HERDSA Guides of which this is one. As part of the updating process, the series editors have stressed the important complementary goals of producing Guides that are highly practical, yet also grounded in evidence-based scholarship.

With these goals in mind, we have approached our task by retaining the original structure of the Guide, which has stood the test of time over two previous editions, while ensuring that its recommendations and suggestions are supported by research evidence, as was the case with the earlier editions. At the same time, our approach is unashamedly practical. Busy academics seeking assistance do not need to be weighed down in a Guide such as this with overly detailed accounts of theory, research, or academic debates around technical issues. References to some excellent sources of further reading are provided for those who wish to explore these matters in more detail.

One of the more recent reviews of lecturing and teaching in large classes in higher education provides support for maintaining the original approach. Mulryan-Kyne (2010) cites a total of 61 sources in her review article on teaching large classes. Of these sources, half were published in the years up to and including 1992 when the last edition of this Guide was written. Only nine have been published since the millennium.

This may suggest that nothing much has changed in our understanding of lecturing. As Mulryan-Kyne's paper shows, comparatively little published work on teaching large classes has appeared since the millennium compared to what came before. And yet so much has changed that affects our work as postsecondary teachers, including major advances in educational technology, differences in the composition of the student body and the increasing calls for accountability, where constant evaluation of teaching is the rule rather than the exception.

Moreover, we are also aware that more research is being done in areas that influence learning and teaching in large classes. Some examples include emotion and learning (Grootenboer, 2010; Hogan & Kwiatkowski, 1998), assessment (Taras, 2010) and its most important cousin, feedback (Bailey & Garner, 2010; Hattie & Timperley, 2007).

More fundamentally, however, changes in the way we think about student learning and how these changes need to be reflected in the way in which we lecture are continuing to have a positive impact on teaching in higher education (Biggs & Tang, 2007; Knapper & Cropley, 2000; Ramsden, 2003). For example, we have taken to heart Ramsden's main message, so clearly set out in the preface to his book, which is to become a good teacher, first understand your student's experience of learning.

We are deeply conscious of criticism often levelled at publications like this. They are often derided as 'cookbooks' or merely 'tips for teachers'. Yet, our cumulative experience over many years in working with new academics suggests that 'mere cookbooks' and 'tips' (we prefer the term 'strategies') are, in fact, very highly valued by beginning teachers – and often by the more experienced as well – people who want to make a positive start in their teaching careers, develop some confidence in teaching and use this basis to embark on a deeper review and development of their initial practices at a later time.

Finally, we have kept the title 'Lecturing' for this revised guide and resisted the temptation to change it to 'large group teaching' – a term that in many ways we believe is more suitable and educationally defensible. The main reasons for maintaining the title is that 'Lecturing' is the original title used in this series and– rightly or wrongly – lecturing is the main teaching method for many academics and therefore the term they are more likely to use when searching for advice and ideas. However, we could not resist the temptation to import the word 'learning' which is now included in the new title. Although we begin with the idea of lecturing, we have taken every opportunity to promote the idea of large group teaching as an approach with a stronger focus on helping students to learn more effectively. Learning, after all, is the sole purpose of all teaching.

We appreciate the feedback that we have received on the ideas and strategies discussed in this Guide from our academic colleagues with whom we have worked over many years in both professional development workshops and on a one-to-one consulting basis in many different countries.

We also wish to thank Allan Goody, HERDSA Guides Editor, for his helpful advice during the revision process, along with the feedback from the HERDSA reviewers of this revised edition.

How To Use This Guide

If you	Then ....
are a complete beginner and have not lectured before...	read the whole Guide and then work through it sequentially as you prepare to lecture.
want to save time in preparing lectures...	read Chapter 2 Lecture Preparation.
want to improve your delivery...	read the section Preparation of the lecture presentation (p. 14) and Chapter 3 Lecture Presentation.
want to make more effective use of audio-visual aids...	read the section Preparation of audio-visual materials (p. 17) and then Use of audio-visual materials (p. 31).
want to obtain some feedback on how your lectures are being received by students...	carry out an evaluation of your lectures using Chapter 4 Evaluation of Lectures as a guide.
want to explore ways of encouraging more effective student learning...	the whole guide is relevant to this need, but Chapter 5 Moving from Teacher Telling to Student Learning in Lectures will be most helpful.
want a full discussion of the research on lectures...	turn to Chapter 6 Recommended Reading that provides some starting resources.

Chapter 1
The Effective Lecturer

The decrying of the wholesale use of lectures is probably justified. The wholesale decrying of the use of lecturing is just as certainly not justified.

R. B. Spence, 1928
If telling was the same as teaching we would all be so smart we could hardly stand it.
R. F. Mager, 1968

INTRODUCTION

Many distinguished scholars have written about lecturing and continue to do so, demonstrating a longstanding interest in the communication of the substantive aspects of disciplines to others.

Michael Faraday (1791-1867), one of the most influential scientists in history, was a proponent of better lecturing. Faraday was only 19 years old when he delivered his first lecture, and an anthology of his writings on lecturing, compiled by the Royal Institution in 1960, contains comprehensive and succinct advice on common concerns such as planning, delivery and personal qualities of the lecturer that are as relevant today as when they were written in the 1800s. Another writer takes us much further back in history, noting that the oldest essay and book ever discovered were treatises on effective speaking and communication, written about 3,000 B.C. for the guidance of the Pharaohs (McCroskey, 1968, p.3).

Our approach in this Guide is to recognise that all university teachers will need to lecture or to give formal presentations at some time in their careers. While we share R. B. Spence's reservations, quoted above, about the ubiquity of the traditional lecture course, we also believe that lectures can be an important component of good teaching, and our aim here is to offer guidance on how to make them as effective as possible for student learning. To give just one example, even for the teacher who wishes to encourage independent learning, lectures can provide a general framework for a course and serve as a guide for exploration of a topic and a discipline.

We also recognise that in many cases individual teachers in higher education have very limited choice but to make lectures a component of their courses. They may be required to lecture because of student numbers and departmental curriculum policies. We hope to help such teachers make their lectures as effective and enjoyable as possible by sharing ideas and strategies for making lectures more active for individual students and interactive among groups of students.

WHY LECTURE?

Conscientious teachers will have thought through the fundamental question 'why lecture?' and arrived at their own conclusions as to why they are engaged in lecturing at all. It is a question that effective lecturers keep under constant review. This is partly because they understand that the evidence supporting lecturing as an effective method of learning and teaching is not strong, and partly because they recognize that constantly enquiring into the effects of their teaching practice on student learning is central to improving both learning and teaching.

Lectures are more or less taken for granted in higher education, but there is abundant evidence that they are comparatively ineffective in promoting the kinds of learning that university academics say they value most: understanding, problem-solving, analysis, and creativity rather than just the acquisition of information. The classic text that discusses this evidence is Donald Bligh's book What's the Use of Lectures?
We take the view that we all have to make presentations from time to time in our professional and academic careers, and that most courses involve some lectures. Some of the currently valid educational reasons why we might lecture include:

- When it is necessary to introduce a whole course or a topic before students undertake further individual or group-based work
- When material is not readily available elsewhere or needs to be organized in a particular way
- When the teacher needs to help students understand alternative points of view, demonstrate particular disciplinary approaches to understanding, analysis or evaluation, or link their own research and experience in insightful ways to student learning
- When the teacher needs to integrate, summarise or evaluate information from a variety of sources such as from sub-group discussions conducted during classtime.

The last point above reminds us of some thought-provoking advice about lectures. That is, to move away from thinking of them as presentations to students towards arranging them as plenaries with students.

Whatever the situation, we can learn how to make our lectures – or plenaries – as clear and as effective as possible. Despite many challenges, the lecture survives. Predictions that the lecture method would fade away have proved to be quite wrong, particularly as most institutions continue to struggle with high student- teacher ratios.

The ideas contained in this Guide are a start in the quest to maintain the quality of teaching in the face of such challenges, and books addressing this matter listed in the Recommended Reading at the end of the Guide should be consulted for further advice and suggestions.

This Guide seeks to offer practical suggestions on lecturing. The ideas are derived partly from an interpretation of the research findings and partly from experience and insights gleaned from working with lecturers and giving many lectures ourselves over the past 50 years!

CHARACTERISTICS OF THE EFFECTIVE LECTURER

Extensive research has identified characteristics that appear to be related to effective teaching in higher education. These same characteristics can be helpful when thinking about lecturing. We consider these characteristics under a number of general headings.

ORGANISATION

Course planning, preparation of a lecture series and of individual lectures, and the use of time are all elements of organisation. Students will be looking for clarity in both the organisation and in the presentation of your course of lectures.

INSTRUCTION

This characteristic describes those interrelated skills such as explaining, demonstrating, discussing, using aids, and the stimulation of thinking.

ASSESSMENT, EVALUATION AND FEEDBACK

It is worth listing assessment, evaluation and feedback separately to emphasise the importance of reliable and valid assessment of student learning and feedback, on the one hand, and evaluation of your own teaching on the other. Unless regular assessment of student understanding is built into teaching (and this does not imply regular class tests, but rather opportunities for students to assess themselves), it will be impossible to work cooperatively and provide constructive feedback to assist students' understanding and to address possible misunderstandings of what they are learning.

RELATIONSHIPS

The quality of relationships with other students and academics is central to the creation of positive learning environments. The ways in which a lecturer relates to students are very important. Evidence of genuine interest in students and their understanding of course material, enthusiasm for the subject, helpfulness, and a sense of humour are qualities that are frequently identified as characteristics of effective teachers. Research also suggests that a narrow focus on lecture content to the exclusion of a genuine consideration of relationships with students is a barren course to follow. Similarly, poor relationships with students or lack of concern for their needs will also affect engagement.

ENGAGEMENT

Sound relationships among students and teachers provide the foundation for student engagement. The greater the personal engagement students have with their academic and non-academic life at university, the greater the likelihood of educational and personal returns on that level of engagement. A key advantage of focusing on engaging students in lectures is that it improves rapport and directs attention towards real understanding. Many researchers have found that student engagement is linked positively to desirable learning outcomes such as critical thinking (Astin, 1999; Carini, Kuh & Klein, 2006; Pascarella & Terenzini, 2005).

SUBJECT KNOWLEDGE

Whilst not denying the importance of an up-to-date knowledge in your own field, it is necessary to counter the prevalent attitude among many academics that this is the only important characteristic of the effective teacher. It is essential to be competent in the other qualities described here as well, and to have a strong commitment to student learning.

These characteristics of the effective lecturer describe minimal effectiveness. In addition, you must be able to achieve planned learning outcomes, such as helping students to understand a concept or to solve problems. This is a good place to review your learning goals.

Chapter 2
Lecture Preparation

INTRODUCTION

We have listed preparation as one of the characteristics of the effective teacher Preparation is a broad concept and goes well beyond the planning of what you intend to say in your lecture. It certainly includes organisation of the subject matter, but also preparation of:

- the presentation of the lecture and any planned student activity
- lecture materials
- the physical environment of the lecture.

Another way of thinking about preparation is under two broad headings:

- management matters in preparing for teaching students
- educational matters that support student learning.

Careful preparation can do a great deal to address issues of lecture effectiveness, student motivation, and your own levels of stress. Accordingly, skills in preparation are worthy of close attention. Of course, you need to be reasonably efficient during the preparatory process to avoid the common pitfall of spending too much time on it. Time-wasting can be due to poor skills in preparation or to procrastination. Both of these problems can be eliminated with a little guidance and some practice. The ideas that follow can be applied to the preparation of a single lecture and, with appropriate modifications, to a series of lectures or a course module.

CONTEXT AND GOALS OF THE LECTURE

An important preliminary step in your preparation is to find out as much as you can about the context of your lectures within the overall program. Unfortunately this context is often ill defined and may be only titles in a long list of lecture topics given out by the teaching department or school.

However, do try to find out as much as you can. This means enquiring about such things as:

- What students have been taught and what they may already know
- The expected goals of your lectures
- What resources, such as library materials, are available for students
- What assessment has been arranged for the course or unit

- Whether the lectures are the only method of teaching or a part of a broader range of methods such as discussion and practical work
- How this lecture or lecture series fits within the structure of the course you're teaching and within the department's broader program
- What methods have been used to teach these students recently.

This last point is most important. You may wish to try out some new ideas with students. But proceed carefully! Students do appreciate good teaching but may resent the use of techniques that seem irrelevant to their purposes, to the course aims, and especially to the way the course is assessed. In introducing new techniques you must carefully explain their purpose to students. Be prepared for some resistance, especially from senior students, if they do not appreciate the connection between the techniques and their past experiences in university and, particularly, the assessment arrangements.

The course controller, curriculum committee, head of department and other lecturers in the course are all potential sources of assistance to you. However, do not be surprised if you are told that you are supposed to be the expert and that it is your responsibility to know what students should be taught! If this happens you should insist on some help to review what happened in the past. To do otherwise is to teach in an academic vacuum.

What is the purpose of the lecture?

Having clarified the context of your lecture you need to ask yourself, What is the purpose of my lecture or series of lectures? This will allow you to have a clear idea about matching ends with means. Think about the question now and make a mental note with reference to a particular lecture or lecture series you are planning.

A possible range of answers is given below, many of which will overlap.

- To **present** students with information about a subject.
  Example: A commentary on the research about an issue.
- To **demonstrate** or model a procedure, a way of thinking, or approach to problem-solving.
  Example: Leading students through a line of reasoning about a problem; demonstrating (with apparatus) a physical phenomenon.
- To **construct an academic argument.**
  Example: Presenting the pro and con arguments.
- To **encourage thinking.**
  Example: Interpretation of a set of data; evaluation of an engineering proposal; criticism of a literary or artistic work, a journal article, or medical treatment plan; application of earlier learning to a novel situation.
- To **guide or motivate.**

Example: Introducing a topic; outlining a series of activities that students are to undertake; providing motivating real-life examples arising from the lecture; offering feedback to students on the basis of assignments they have completed.

Resolving the purpose of the lecture will provide a useful benchmark throughout the process of lecture preparation, presentation and final evaluation. Of course, the specific purpose of a lecture will have a large influence on the way that lecture will be prepared. For example, a feedback lecture will require a very different approach to one where you purposely set out to encourage students to think about something new. You may wish to begin by assessing students' initial course-related understanding or attitudes and some ways of doing this are described below. Frequently, however, the goal of the lecture will be related to some kind of subject matter or course content and so we use this as a starting point for considering lecture preparation.

SELECTION AND PREPARATION OF SUBJECT MATTER

'Subject matter' is the information, ideas, interpretations, analyses, arguments, examples, evidence, assumptions, problems, and solutions, for your lecture. Selecting subject matter can be troublesome and time-consuming, especially for the beginner. The following suggestions are presented as ideas to get you started.

PREPARING A SUBJECT MATTER OUTLINE

Many lecturers admit that their lecture preparation is frequently characterised by procrastination, confusion or 'lecturer's block'. The technique of free-association may assist in addressing these difficulties.

Free-association is an idea-generating technique. To begin, do not be concerned about the order in which ideas will eventually be presented in your lecture. Start the free-association process by writing the lecture topic and purpose in the centre of a sheet of paper. Then think about the lecture. As ideas, facts, questions, possible student activities, and sources of information come to mind, note these down. When ideas are identified these will tend to trigger other related ideas. Note these down as well as branches of the main ideas. The diagram below illustrates a way of noting ideas that many lecturers find helpful.

This process of free-association may seem a little unusual, but try this process once or twice to determine its suitability for your needs. Many lecturers have found it to be very helpful.

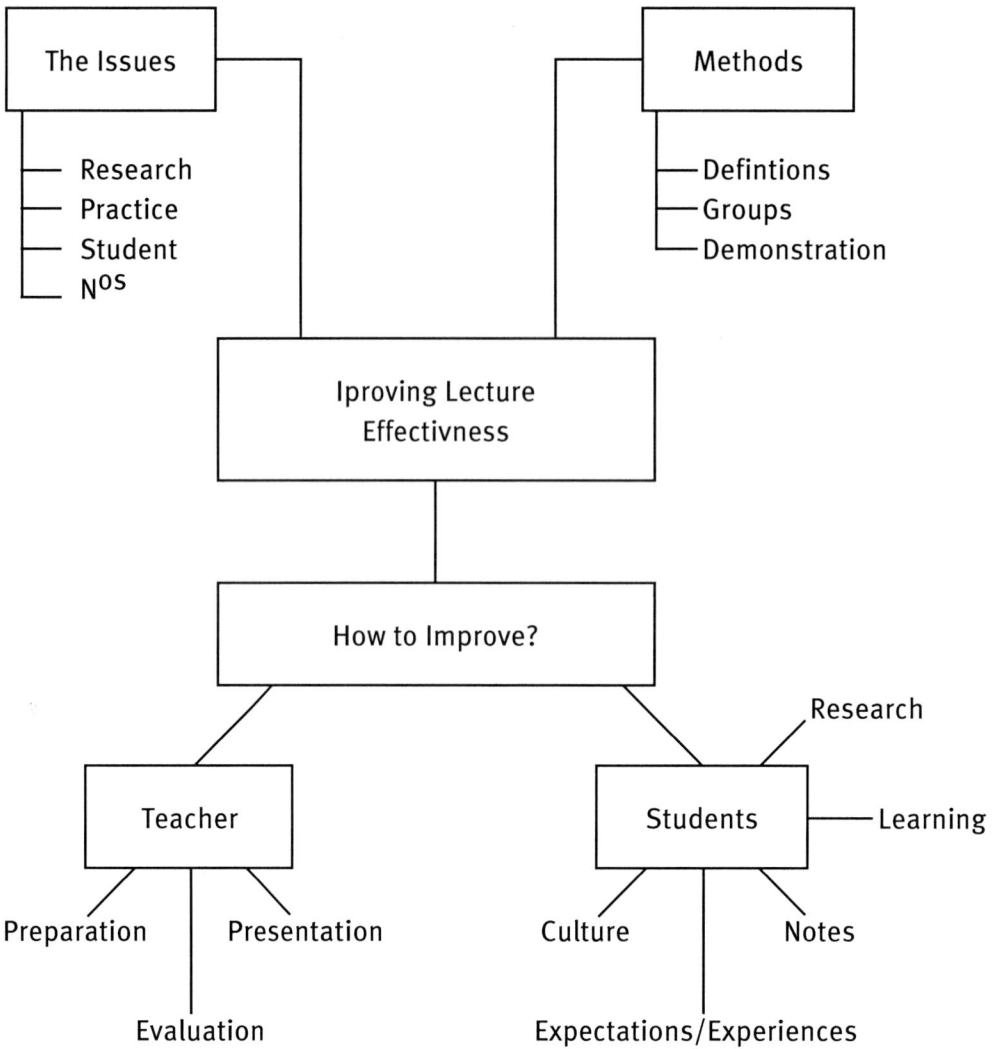

The lecture topic, in this case, improving lecture effectiveness, is placed in the centre and you can then note ideas around it, as illustrated. You should write down your main ideas 'off the top of your head' before you start detailed reading on the topic, or else you run the risk of getting overwhelmed by information. Indeed, your reading and research should be guided and focused by the outline you are preparing.

You will probably supplement these ideas from further reading suggested by your initial ideas, but also ask yourself how your subject matter can be selected to motivate and interest your students. The following prompts are suggested ways of achieving interest and motivation:

- avoid quantity – 'covering' too much material at the expense of achieving depth; much better to 'uncover' student understandings and address these in the lecture
- use everyday situations such as may be found in newspapers, on the web and

television, through students' experiences or from locally available materials to explain relationships between phenomena

- demonstrate the practical applications of recent research in stimulating ways link theory and practice, or better still, challenge students to derive theories from their own observations
- show how different ideas, concepts, and theories are connected and can be integrated
- explore common student misconceptions
- try to build on students' natural curiosity.

A challenging question to keep in mind here is, What can I leave out to improve student interest and understanding – in other words, how much is enough? Commonly, too much material is packed into a lecture, which often defeats the purpose of helping students to learn. Just because the lecturer has presented material does not mean that students truly comprehend it. Aim for quality learning, not information quantity!

As you associate ideas, be careful not to limit your thinking to what we shall call your 'expert view'. Do not assume that students know and believe what you do. Try to find ways to enter the topic, problem or concept from the learner's perspective. Here, students' responses to assignments and tests can be a source of rich information about their misconceptions that can be used for teaching. Regular and informal discussions with students will yield further information. To illustrate, a study of misconceptions in physical science among undergraduate students found students referring incorrectly to 'atoms of sugar' but then correctly to 'molecules of water' with no apparent understanding of the meaning of the terms or of the differences between them. Further, some students thought a drop of water contained one molecule, rather than billions (Linke & Venz, 1978). Clearly, these kinds of scientific misconceptions require much more attention in a teaching program on the structure of matter.

Your experience of teaching will provide some insights into students' misconceptions of your subject and potential sources of difficulty because of their varied backgrounds. Reflect carefully on the backgrounds of your students. It is likely that many will have come from overseas or from non-English speaking families. And there will be both men and women in your class. In this situation you must give careful consideration to the selection of examples you plan to use in your lectures so that all present have a reasonable chance to relate to them. In other words, your examples must not be so culture or gender-specific that all students cannot be reasonably expected to understand them.

This does not imply being so general as to be bland: by all means give examples and illustrations from your personal experience, which most students will welcome. But put them into context, and perhaps invite students to offer examples from their own experiences.

Another way of proceeding is to discuss concepts with students to explore their understanding and possible mistaken beliefs. Inspection of examination scripts and submitted work from past and present students can be illuminating. This type of information can be useful in building up a teaching strategy, and can be used directly as data for examples and illustrations in future lectures and tutorials.

FINALISING THE SUBJECT MATTER PLAN

Eventually you will have to transform your ideas into some kind of structure. You should do this after you have completed any necessary reading or data gathering suggested by your rough outline and after you have edited your ideas. There are several structures you can use to organise your ideas.

At the most elementary level is the old rule of thumb in teaching which says, Tell them what you are going to tell them, tell them, and then tell them what you told them! Since we have already criticised simple 'telling' behaviour as a means of teaching, we should really translate this rule into a more educationally acceptable structure. A basic form is:

- Introduction and overview
- Main points of lecture
- Review of main points and conclusion.

A more developed version of this structure is:
- Introduction and Overview
- Purpose and context of lecture
- Overview of main points of lecture
- Revision of earlier material, links to previous lectures; common student misunderstandings and concerns with the material
- Perhaps a short activity as a way of discovering what students know and believe when they start the lecture/course/module.
- First Main Point
- Development and explanation of ideas
- Examples
- Restatement of first point.
- Second Main Point
- Development and explanation of ideas
- Examples
- Restatement of first and second points.
- Third/Fourth Main Points
- As above.
- Summary and Conclusion
- Restatement and   review of main points
- Student activity, linked to activity in 1, above, to assess understanding
- Conclusion or implications
- Details of next lecture, preparation, etc.

This structure is probably the easiest to plan but least engaging for students. However, this type of structure can be adapted to other lecture purposes. Let us consider two examples. The first example is called the **comparative** structure.

If you wished to lecture on the comparisons between A and B you could start with:

- **Introduction**
- **First major point:** Details about A
- **Second major point:** Details about B
- **Third major point:** Criteria for comparison
- **Fourth major point:** Comparisons and contrasts
- **Summary and Conclusions:** Perhaps supplemented by some activity to assess student understanding.

A second adaptation of the basic structure is for a lecture that is problem-focused. It can be structured as follows:

- **Introduction:** Statement of the problem and overview of range of solutions
- **First major point:** Solution I
- **Second major point:** Solution II
- **Third major point:** Solution III
- **Fourth major point:** Comparison in terms of simplicity, validity, or appropriateness
- **Summary and Conclusions.**

The third adaptation is the **academic-argument** structure. The order in which you place arguments in this structure appears to be critical. Andrews (2010) discusses ways in which arguments can be developed and presented and his book is recommended as a helpful resource. A suggested order is:
- **Introduction:** Overview of lecturer's position and supporting arguments
- **First major point:** Counter-arguments
- **Second major point:** Critique of counter-arguments and evidence
- **Third major point:** Arguments in favour of lecturer's position and evidence
- **Conclusion:** Restatement of lecturer's position.

Of course the main purpose of higher education is not to evangelise or propagandise, so with this approach it will be important to offer students the opportunity to debate and argue, either in class or in a following tutorial. The problem-centred and academic-argument structures are potentially much more engaging which is why the approaches are often used in television documentaries.

Examples here may imply that lectures are complete in themselves. In reality, of course, this is rarely the case. Most lectures will be part of a lecture series on a particular topic or theme. Consequently, they will need to be linked together to provide continuity from one lecture to the next. In this case, the introduction provides the opportunity to help students refresh their understanding from the previous lecture. Similarly, and rather than ending a lecture in 'mid-air', it is appropriate to provide at least a few closing comments, which may include a review of the material presented plus an overview of what is to come in the next lecture. In other words, you will need to modify the structures suggested above to suit the demands of your teaching as it proceeds from one lecture to the next.

Finally, by constantly thinking about your lectures in terms of what students understand – by reviewing understanding at the beginning of a lecture and by conducting simple activities and self-assessment tasks during or at the end of a lecture – you help move your own and students' perceptions away from lectures as a method of 'delivering information' towards understanding and learning.

The structures described above illustrate the general question you will have to answer as you organize your material, which is How will I sequence the ideas I wish to present? Sometimes – but by no means always – the sequence might be dictated by the nature of the material to be presented. This could be the case if you were presenting the sequence of events leading to a particular discovery. However, apparently logical sequences may not always be optimal for student learning, and you should give some thought to the ways in which student interests, knowledge, and approaches to problems suggest sequences of presentation. Some possible sequences are to proceed:

- From simple ideas and applications to more complex ones
- From what students can be expected to know to what students do not know
- From common misconceptions among students to explanation and clarification
- From observations of reality (e.g. a case study, a visit earlier in the course, a news item, a short video, a role play, a demonstration) to abstract ideas, theories and principles. This is called an inductive approach to teaching
- From generalisations to particular examples and applications. This is a deductive approach – a reversal of the inductive sequence outlined above
- From a whole view to a more detailed view and then back to the whole view.

PREPARATION OF THE LECTURE PRESENTATION

As you think about the subject-matter of the lecture you will generate questions and ideas about how to present your lecture and engage students. Make sure to make a note of these questions and ideas as they occur to you, perhaps on the rough outline, but in a different colour to distinguish them from your subject- matter concerns.

Experience shows that there are many things to consider in a lecture delivery. It is difficult to identify all of these because so many will be context-specific, depending, for instance, on the freedom you have to determine exactly how and what you teach, where you teach, the numbers of students and their characteristics, and so on. There are, however, some aspects of lecture presentation that should always be considered during your preparation. Fundamental support for your presentation will be in the form of your own notes. These means of support are considered below.

BEGINNINGS AND ENDINGS

Some lecturers have difficulty making appropriate opening and closing remarks and make the mistake of composing them on-the-spot. This strategy often fails and can unnecessarily increase your feelings of anxiety. There can be several consequences of this failure: essential information may be omitted, nervousness and uncertainty may be communicated leading to loss of control of the class, and an opportunity to create interest may be missed. The preparation of your beginning should include consideration of what you will actually say in the first few sentences, comments you might make about previous work or lectures, and what you will do with teaching materials such as the distribution of handouts, the function of PowerPoint slides and whiteboard outlines.

The following are some ways to plan a beginning.

- **Make links** to previous work completed by students, known interests and concerns of students, or to topical issues (such as a recent and relevant news report)
- **Explain the structure:** simple, clear statements, preferably written on the board or on a slide, about the structure of the lecture are a helpful beginning and point-of-reference during a lecture
- **Create visual interest:** showing a slide, short segment of video, or a model can create interest and stimulate thinking
- **State the problem:** display or state the problem that will be addressed during the lecture.

We have found it well-received to both start and end a lecture with a summary of the main points or headings and with links to previous and following lectures. Of course, you can combine two or more of these ways of beginning if you wish. One benefit in using some kind of visual display at the beginning is that it directs attention to the visual aid rather than to you. This allows you to settle into the lecture and can help overcome the distressing breathlessness that is sometimes experienced early in a lecture delivery.

Endings should also be carefully planned. They should reflect the kinds of decisions made in the outline structure and should provide clear conclusions to the lecture. Avoid entering into a verbal battle against a rising level of noise at the end of the session. If necessary, pause and insist on silence, until you reach your planned conclusion (but of course this can only be effective as long as you have not run over the allotted time)! Again you will find it helpful to have a prepared form of words to end your lecture.

As you prepare your lecture, you will also need to think about varying your presentation. Chapter 3 Lecture Presentation provides some examples of how you might go about doing this.

NOTES FOR YOUR LECTURE

It is rarely desirable or justifiable to read a lecture directly from a script particularly when material can be easily provided to students via the web. A lecture is not a formal speech.

Reading a lecture breaks down contact with your students and reduces the likelihood of engaging their interest in the lecture material. It is also quite easy to lose your place in a prepared script, particularly if you need to respond to a student questions. At the same time, you will need notes to guide you through your lecture and provide helpful prompts. Here are some ways of preparing notes we have found helpful.

Method 1

Write out your major headings and points on cards and arrange these in an appropriate sequence. Some cards could be colour-coded to indicate important transitions in your presentation: a green card and its contents may indicate use of slides; an orange card, small group activity with students; and so on. If cards are used, ensure they are numbered clearly: the consequences of not doing so are obvious!

Method 2

Write out your notes on sheets of paper or use the 'Notes' or 'Handout' facility in PowerPoint to provide the outline you need. Use generous margins, and have clear, bold headings that you will be able to see easily when teaching. Avoid the temptation to write down every detail of content. As well as writing down the major points of your subject-matter content, be sure to indicate the learning activities you will use: for example, 'show first two slides', 'write title on whiteboard', or 'students to read handout'.

Personal presentation reminders to yourself can also be inserted: 'smile'; 'slow down'; 'pause'; 'look to the left – right – back'; and so on.

Method 3

This is an extension of Method 2 and is suggested when PowerPoint or an overhead projector is used extensively. Notes are interspersed with hard copies of the slides or overhead transparencies, extracts from books, single copies of handouts to be distributed at various stages, and so on. The stack of material thus created is then worked through systematically. There is little risk of losing your place in a lecture when using this method as long as you keep your material in order.

Whichever method of preparing lecture notes is chosen, it is important that you should feel comfortable and happy with it – and so should your students! If a method is not helpful for some reason, another should be tried until you find one that suits your own style of teaching.

THE USE OF HUMOUR IN LECTURES

There is very good evidence of the psychological and physiological benefits of humour and laughter. The psychological effects include decreased anxiety and stress, improved self-esteem, increased motivation, and higher perceived quality of life. Extensive physiological benefits have been documented for the muscular, respiratory, cardiovascular, endocrine, immune, and central nervous systems. Of particular relevance to the nervous lecturer, humour has been found to relax muscles, decrease pain and lower pulse rate and blood pressure (Berk, 1996). Studies of the characteristics of successful teachers have shown the importance of using humour in the classroom (Powell & Andresen, 1985) and others find that students see humour as an effective tool to facilitate their learning (Berk, 1996; Murray, 1991).

Many of us are not naturally funny people, but it is possible to plan for the use of humour in our lectures. Done properly – an important caveat – humour can create a pleasant atmosphere in which to teach and this, in itself, is a strong reason to use it. Even more important is the evidence that humour can actually reinforce learning.

Many people find it difficult to recall humorous stories or jokes or to find suitable material for use in lectures. One solution is to start a collection of humour for teaching purposes: file away cartoons, stories, jokes, quotations and the like that you come across in your reading and day-to-day affairs. Professional journals and magazines will sometimes have suitable material, as will web sites, the daily press, weekly magazines, desk pads, and diaries. You can buy books on general humour and anthologies of jokes that can be easily modified to suit your needs. Whole books of specific discipline-based humour are beginning to appear in some subjects, such as philosophy (Cathcart & Klein, 2007), so it may be worth checking publication lists and web sites for material in your field.

Finally, there are numerous sources of humour on the web of which just three examples are provided here: *The Journal of Irreproducible Results* (http://www.jir. com/), *The Journal of Nursing Jocularity* (http://www.journalofnursingjocularity.com/) and *The International Society for Humor Studies* (http://www.hnu.edu/ishs/).
Another approach to finding suitable humour to use in teaching is to offer examples and materials about yourself, especially humorous anecdotes that bear on the topics being presented.

You must be sensitive in selecting the kind of humour that is relevant to your social context and be cautious of becoming known as a clown by over-using humour. An even more serious matter is to be thoroughly careful with the kind of humour you use. Never, ever, use material in teaching that is remotely likely to offend some members of your class. Racist, sexist, sexual, religious, and sick humour, all come into this category. You may get a cheap laugh. But you will damage the academic relationships that you are trying to establish with at least some of your students, and that is a risk not worth taking.

Finally, you should plan when to use humour in your lecture. You could use humour at the beginning of the lecture to aid in establishing rapport with your students or to illustrate a point you will develop later. You could use humorous material to provide an example of something you have been discussing or to lead on to a new point. And you can use humour during the ending of your lecture. As your skill and confidence grows you may be able to also use humour spontaneously!

PREPARATION OF AUDIO-VISUAL MATERIALS

This section is rather lengthy for an important reason: many lecturers use audio- visual materials either poorly, or not at all, when with some thought and planning they could have been used to very good effect. Further, it can be said that far too many audio-visual aids offend the common sense rule that 'visual aids should be visible and audio aids should be audible'!

Audio-visual materials may be used to help achieve a number of purposes in your lecture. These include:

- introducing your lecture, or parts of it
- providing illustrative examples of the material being discussed
- presenting material that is unsuitable or too complex for words
- stimulating interest, thought, or discussion on a topic
- providing variety or to 'break up' a presentation (and thus contribute to
- engaging the attention and interest of students)
- summarising or integrating ideas presented
- assisting in the communication process with overseas and non-English speaking students.

Careful consideration of the purpose of your lecture, the information that is best presented using audio-visual media, and ways of providing suitable variety and structure will help in deciding upon appropriate media.

Before you start lecturing, you should take time to check the availability of audio- visual support services in your institution and, in particular, the technological resources that are provided where you will be teaching. At the very least, take some time before you meet your class to become thoroughly familiar with the operation of these resources. Conversely, never attempt to master complicated facilities in lecture theatres at the same time that your lecture begins!

You might consider using one or more of the following media in your lecture, although to use all on any one occasion may be a bit much!

- whiteboard (and less commonly these days, the chalkboard), and interactive whiteboards
- PowerPoint and other presentation software
- video
- sound recordings
- other media such as charts, maps, or models
- handouts.

THE WHITEBOARD OR CHALKBOARD

Despite the widespread availability of sophisticated electronic devices, most university lecture rooms are still equipped with boards and, if used properly, they can offer the advantages of spontaneity and flexibility, for example to note down student responses to a question or problem you have posed during the lecture

The presentation of board material should be of sufficient quality to be clearly visible and to assist student note taking. If board-work is an important part of your lecture, its effectiveness can be enhanced by preparing a simple plan worked out on a sheet of paper that should be included among your lecture notes. The sheet should be ruled up into vertical sections to represent the board space you will be using. Each section can then be designated to serve a specific purpose. For example, one section might be used for a brief outline of the structure of the lecture, another section for the development of diagrams, and another for a list of new terms and definitions. An outline of the material you plan to place on the board should then be made on each section of your board plan.

Interactive whiteboards, known as Smart Boards or by other brand names, are sometimes used as a replacement for traditional whiteboards, chalkboards or flipcharts. They provide ways to show students anything that can be presented on a computer's desktop and operate as part of a system that includes the interactive whiteboard, a computer, projector and white board software. If these boards are available in your institution you should seek specialist help in exploring their operation and potential for teaching in your subject.

POWERPOINT

Preparing teaching material using one of a number of available software products can add engaging visual impact to your teaching materials. For simplicity, the term 'PowerPoint' is used here in a generic sense to describe the range of presentation software products which also includes Apple Keynote and OpenOffice. Its use in this way is in no way intended as an endorsement for this particular product.

Used wisely and following a few simple guidelines, PowerPoint can be an effective resource to support your lecture. You can embed video and audio files, animations, illustrations, art and photos into slides with relative ease. Within the program itself, you can create many types of graphics such as organization charts, lists and picture diagrams. If the classroom is connected to the Internet, embedding hyperlinks into your slides enables you to access other resources and documents.

There are many how-to-do-it guides readily available in libraries and bookshops on preparing and using PowerPoint presentations of which guides in the For Dummies series are just one example (http://au.wiley.com/WileyCDA). A Google search of the web will produce an additional and bewildering array of information on PowerPoint. Basic principles are also available on Microsoft's own web site (http:// office.microsoft.com/en-au/ powerpoint-help) from where some of the following key guidelines have been developed:

- Keep the number of slides to a minimum and focus on essential
- As a guide for student attention and understanding, keep the visual presentation simple and consistent, with subtle templates or themes and easy-to-read text; avoid complex slide designs, statements, and data sets, and distracting special effectsFocus on the legibility of your slides: use one family of typeface and one that will be found on most computers such as Arial, Helvetica or Times so that your layout remains stable from one computer to another; use lowercase lettering that is easy to read; font size should be large enough when projected to be read from the back of large lecture theatres and this means about 48 points for headings, 30 points for the body, and no more than about 45 characters, including spaces, per line. Create a few slides with a variety of font sizes and colours and check these out in a lecture theatre at some time to review legibility criteria
- Reduce tabulated data to essential and rounded figures, or better still convert it to a graphical form – usually, a simple graph will be very much more effective in communicating an idea
- If using text and bullet points, consider the '666 Rule' – never more than 6 consecutive slides of text; no more than 6 bullet points per slide; no more than 6 words per bullet pointMatch backgrounds and text for legibility such as black text on white or white

  against dark blue; avoid red text and pale colours that will be difficult – if not impossible – to read when projected
- Maximize the visual character of the medium with graphics such charts, diagrams, cartoons, and pictures whenever possible.

Remember that PowerPoint is only a visual aid to what you are doing; it is not the lecture itself. This means that your lecture material does not have to be 'dumbed- down' to the simple layout recommendations set out here. You will often need to supplement your slides with references to texts and other resources or to a printed handout. Remember too that

PowerPoint and similar presentation software is designed primarily for use in business, not educational settings, and you need to adapt it accordingly.

Much of what might be considered lecture material in the form of PowerPoint presentations can now be published to the web using software such as Adobe Presenter. This enables you to integrate other media including audio, video, simulations, tests and feedback and potentially makes much of the need for traditional lecturing for transmitting information redundant. Seek advice from teaching support services or their web site on how to do this.

A note of caution is appropriate here. The use of PowerPoint technology has become so widespread in education that serious concerns have been raised about its impact. There are very strong critiques of PowerPoint and we suggest that you familiarise yourself with these to help you develop a balanced use of this technology in your teaching – if you intend to use it at all. PowerPoint is seen by some as facilitating the very worst kind of teaching through its attempts to reduce complex and interesting concepts to tedious and simplistic hierarchies and bullet-points, with far too much material presented at high speed sometimes with unnecessary and distracting visual gimmicks such as spinning text and an emphasis on 'covering' the material at the expense of deeper understanding.

A leading critic of this type of presentation technology has been Edward Tufte (2006). An introduction to his concerns can be found on Wikipedia and in the article *PowerPoint is Evil* available at http://www.wired.com/wired/archive/11.09/ ppt2.html.

Some of Tufte's concerns with PowerPoint, relevant to its use for learning and teaching, focus on these ideas:
- PowerPoint is evolving more as a guide for the presenter than a means to increase student understanding
- Ideas are often arranged in deep hierarchies and the meaning for students is lost in that hierarchy
- PowerPoint forces a linear progression through the hierarchy, whereas a handout or reference to a text allows browsing and the facility to return to a statement
- Simplistic, linear thinking is encouraged by the nature of PowerPoint and the over-use of its bulleted lists
- Poor typography and layouts prepared by novice users may lead to almost useless presentations.

Tufte's article raises a thought-provoking question for teachers concerned about developing good relationships and student understanding: *PowerPoint's pushy style seeks to set up a speaker's dominance over the audience. The speaker, after all, is making 'power points' with 'bullets' to followers. Could any metaphor be worse?*

OVERHEAD TRANSPARENCIES

Although largely overtaken by the ubiquitous availability of PowerPoint, the overhead projector (one of the very few communication technologies developed originally for educational use) is still in wide use and so a few words about this device are appropriate. The overhead projector can project a variety of transparency material, silhouettes of opaque objects, and animated devices on to a screen.

The most common application of the overhead projector is to show material prepared on transparencies using clear acetate sheets and special felt pens (felt pens used for writing on paper are generally not suitable). Information can be handwritten, printed, or drawn directly on to the acetate sheet. A suggested procedure is to mount the acetate sheet onto a cardboard frame with adhesive tape, place a piece of graph paper underneath the acetate as a writing guide, and then write directly on to the acetate. Another way of preparing transparencies is to use a software package to generate the material you need and photocopy onto the transparency, but this raises the possibility of using PowerPoint instead.

When using overhead transparencies in large lecture theatres, it is essential to use large lettering in a dark colour (again, avoiding red), preferably about 5 – 10mm in height. Lettering at least 5mm high will be satisfactory for transparencies to be used in smaller rooms. Apart from being essential for visibility, large lettering has the added advantage - for students - of limiting the amount of information on any one transparency. This makes their reading and noting much more effective. The importance of lettering size and clarity cannot be over-stressed.

DOCUMENT CAMERAS

Some classrooms are now equipped with document cameras (also known as visualisers). Document cameras are real-time image capture devices that project images of text and three-dimensional objects. They provide greater flexibility than overhead projectors by eliminating the need (and cost) to create transparencies; you can use the page of a book or already prepared material. You can write on a piece of paper as you would on transparencies, even freeze-framing the image until you have completed your work before showing the class. An added advantage is that you can zoom in and out on text or on objects to provide close-up detail to your students or view the objects from different angles by moving an object around. This may eliminate the need to pass an object around the class so students can get a closer view.

As with all projected images, it is essential to ensure that the writing, text and objects are sufficiently large and clear to be able to be seen at the back of the lecture theatre. Legibility on a printed page is no guarantee at all of legibility of the projected image of that same page, and so great care is needed when using these cameras. In fact, because text on the printed page was never intended for projection, it is wise not to use document cameras for this purpose at all. Use them for objects, photographs and graphic materials especially prepared for projection.

FILM, VIDEO AND SOUND RECORDINGS

Although it is uncommon to use all of a film or video in a lecture, this can be important for some purposes. For example, a recent study showed how 'movies' can increase student interest in course content at the same time as developing critical thinking (Kennedy, Senses & Ayan, 2011). Short segments of five to ten minutes are generally more effective in facilitating learning than longer screenings and these short segments can be incorporated into a PowerPoint presentation (but make sure you have a means of transmitting sound from the controlling computer). Brief sound recordings can also be a useful supplement in lectures to add variety, provide examples or serve as the basis for discussion.

Depending on the purpose of your lecture, learning from these media will be enhanced by:

- repeating the material if short segments are used
- providing relevant introductions and summaries
- posing questions or setting tasks for consideration during the presentation and for discussion afterwards.

When film, video or audio is being planned, it is important to ensure that all equipment is working properly and that viewing and listening conditions are satisfactory before the presentation commences. The first time you use such media in a new setting try the system out in advance, and go to the back of the room to make sure that visuals can be seen and audio can be heard. More information on the actual use of audio-visual material in the lecture can be found in Chapter 3, Lecture Presentation.

OTHER MEDIA

Maps, charts, real objects, models and specimens can often be used to good effect. Think about these questions in advance:

- Is the material large enough to be seen by all members of the audience? Are objects or specimens to be passed around among the audience? (If yes, the time needed for this will require careful planning indeed to avoid having part of the audience listening to the presentation while others are busy looking at your specimens.)
- Are suitable display surfaces available (e.g., hanging space and hooks for maps, benches for models, specimens, etc.)?

HANDOUTS

Even in the era of the web, many lecturers still use handouts, both for use during the lecture itself, or to be taken away and consulted later. Handouts are generally quick and easy to prepare, but to be used most effectively they deserve careful planning and design. Your first consideration should be to clarify the purpose of using a handout, for example:

- to list lecture aims and objectives to present information – for example, information given in a handout can release time for discussion or for thinking about the application of information, its validity, and its possible connection to other topics discussed in the course to provide a guide to the lecture, its structure and key components – something that will be particularly useful to students if the presentation is complex as a framework to guide note-taking – for example, when films or photographic
- slides are used to present information, handouts can be helpful to provide a summary
- as a guide to stimulate and direct subsequent reading.

An understanding of the purpose of the handout will help decide when you should distribute it. Handouts designed as guides, with blank spaces for notes such as those provided by PowerPoint, should be given out at the beginning of the presentation. Unless notes or reading lists are to be used in the presentation, it is probably preferable to distribute them near the end, but not when people are leaving, so that a few minutes are available for explanation and discussion of their purposes. The critical point here is that if you go to the trouble of preparing handouts, do ensure that you actually use them in the lecture. Simply distributing an unexplained handout at the end of your lecture is a waste of time and materials.

PREPARATION OF THE PHYSICAL ENVIRONMENT

All your efforts at preparing your content, presentation, audio-visuals, notes, and so on can be wasted if you do not give some thought to the room or theatre you will be lecturing in. Of course, you will get to know a particular venue fairly well if you use it regularly, but even in this case it is wise to prepare and check the room for what you want to do. Showing a genuine concern for students' comfort and their working environment contributes to maintaining a good relationship. A checklist of things to consider would include at least the following:

- Seating: Sufficient for numbers expected? Arranged in an appropriate fashion?
- Heating/cooling/ventilation: Appropriately adjusted?
- Audio-visual equipment: In working order? Clean? Correctly located? Can all students see and hear? Pointer available?
- Whiteboard/chalkboard: Clean? Appropriate and sufficient pens or chalk and eraser available?

Your primary considerations in preparing the physical environment will be the comfort of your students and whether you can do the kinds of things you plan to do in the room allocated.

SOME PERSONAL CONSIDERATIONS

When you are satisfied that you have attended adequately to the kinds of things discussed above, you will find it helpful to reflect on some matters of personal preparation for your lecture. Paramount among these considerations is dealing with nervousness - both before and during your lecture.

If you are thoroughly prepared and feel in control of the physical environment, most of the potential sources for nervousness will have been addressed. Keep in mind that a certain level of anxiety is desirable to ensure that you teach well. Most accomplished lecturers, speakers, performers and actors confess to feeling anxious before 'going on-stage', but curiously this does not always manifest itself in the ways that the less experienced imagine. There is a saying that there are two kinds of speakers: those that admit to feelings of anxiety, ... and liars!

Apart from being thoroughly prepared for your lecture, there are a number of 'do's and don'ts' to keep in mind:

- Think positively about the lecture. Imagine an appreciative audience, achievement of the goals you set for students and yourself, and being in control. The secret is to be prepared to the best of your ability – this is one of the best things you can do to instil self-confidence. Do not allow yourself to conjure up visions of mistakes and disasters in your lecture.
- Spend a quiet ten minutes before the lecture for composure and allow no interruptions during this time. Some lecturers practice relaxation exercises and deep breathing. Consult a suitable reference on this topic or attend a relaxation class if you think it might help. If your anxiety is a major concern to you, consider consulting a professional for assistance.
- Listen to relaxing music. Baroque music with a slow restful temp seems to be particularly suitable for this purpose.
- If you can, always plan on arriving at the lecture room early to ensure everything is in order and to allow time to talk to a few students in the class about their work. This approach contributes to your sense of control of the coming lecture and can be helpful in meeting some of the students' needs and in understanding their difficulties that you might be able to use in your lecturing.

All lecturers will find it helpful to practise articulation and voice-projection exercises. Your students who come from non-English speaking backgrounds will also appreciate this activity! Just as we exercise before physical exercise or sport, so too should we exercise our voices before lecturing. Think about pacing (not going too fast for your and your students' own good), articulation (speaking carefully and clearly as if to a foreigner), and avoiding slang and unnecessary jargon. Rehearsal with a tape-recorder or in front of a friend or colleague may be helpful.

Chapter 3
Lecture Presentation

If you have followed our advice so far, by the time you stand up to lecture much of the hard work will have been done. Your task then is to translate your preparation into an educationally worthwhile and pleasing presentation.

STARTING THE LECTURE

For many, this is the most difficult part. It is important, as we have indicated previously, to have a clear idea of how you intend to start before you face your students.

When you have checked your notes, verified that projection systems actually work, cleaned the board and attended to other preliminary matters, go to the lectern, look at the students and wait for silence. If you need to attract attention and obtain silence consider ringing a small counter-bell, displaying a slide or writing up the heading and structure of the lecture on the board. Be firm, but avoid aggressive or pleading moves such as 'Shut-up!' or 'Will you please be quiet?' Only when you have the attention of students should you start with your prepared preliminaries. Look directly at students, and smile to convey your confidence and enthusiasm for your subject (even if you are secretly wanting to be somewhere else!). Looking at the back wall because it is cool and unreactive, or somewhere into space, conveys the wrong message to students.

SPEECH

Speak more slowly than normal. Students, particularly those from non-English speaking backgrounds, will appreciate this and a fast delivery will make understanding of new material and note-taking difficult for all.

As you speak, take time to indicate some verbal 'signposts'. Examples are 'This point is most important', 'The next issue we need to consider is ...', 'So far, we have considered two solutions to the problem. The first solution focused on ... and the second solution stressed ... ' (Notice in the last example how redundancy is used to make it quite clear what is being referred to - the word 'solution' is used rather than vague words such as 'these', 'those', 'that' or 'this'.)

When speaking, consider the virtues of variety - vary the volume and speed of delivery, and use pauses or silence to add emphasis or to gain attention. Suddenly lowering your voice is more likely to attract attention than raising it. Keep in mind the suggestions made earlier about pacing and articulation and, as you speak, avoid the temptation to use jargon and to make the subject more difficult than it needs to be. Use simple language as much as you can. Technical terms should only be used after they have been carefully introduced and explained.

VARIETY

Purely oral lectures often lead to student inattention and boredom. Introducing some variety in your presentation can help overcome this problem. Murray (1991) has a list of behaviours that his research has shown distinguish effective and ineffective lecturers. The list also illustrates variations that can be used successfully when lecturing:

• Speaking expressively or emphatically
• Using appropriate humour
• Showing facial expression rather than keeping your head down behind the lectern
• Showing concern for students, for example, by responding constructively to questions
• Encouraging questions, comments and feedback
• Moving about when lecturing but not to the point of distracting students
• Praising students for good ideas
• Asking questions of the class
• Being friendly and easy to talk to.

There are broadly four kinds of variety and you will find it helpful to prepare for the use of each in your lectures. The following lists some common forms of variety used by lecturers.

EXAMPLES OF VARIETY IN LECTURES

Variation	Purpose
Group 1: Variations in Non-verbal Communication	
Gestures with hands or body	To add emphasis, create interest, attract or to maintain attention
Distributing eye-contact	Establishes 'contact' with students, helps to overcome nervousness

Movement away from lectern	Helps create different atmosphere for less formal aspects of delivery, e.g. asides, humour and dealing with questions. Consider moving among the students to establish personal contact with them
Group 2: Variations in Verbal Communication	
Voice: volume, pitch, speed, resonance	To add emphasis, create interest, or to maintain attention
Pauses or silence, 'word-pictures', humour, asides	Creates interest, provides break from content-laden explanations or reasoning; adds emphasis; humour can create an emotionally pleasant atmosphere for all
Examples, illustrations, quoting from texts, journals, current news items, web pages	Provides interest, authenticity, relevance, topicality, enhanced clarity
Repeating or restating a point in a different way	Adds emphasis to a major point; repetition is an important aid to learning in oral communication where information can easily be missed
One-to-one discussion or small group discussion*	Social purposes can be achieved in addition to intellectual ones
Setting a brief task: quiet period of reading from handout/text; short quiz; problem solving*	Encourages thinking and the development of intellectual skills; opportunity to provide feedback to students

* Refer to Chapter 5 Moving from Teacher Telling to Student Learning in Lectures for further elaboration of these suggestions. Additional practical advice on using discussion techniques is available in the HERDSA Guide Conducting Tutorials by Lublin and Sutherland (2009).

Group 3: Variations in Media of Presentation	
Handouts and copies of slides	For essential definitions, formulae, references; to give structure for note-taking; to provide information not readily available elsewhere
Audio-visual aids such as PowerPoint slides, short 'trigger' videos, models, objects and specimens	To stimulate interest; guide note-taking (using (PowerPoint); provide examples and illustrations (videos,slides, models); provoke discussion (short 'trigger' videos)
Visiting speaker	To add authenticity of direct experience

Concerning the last point, a note of caution is warranted. Visiting speakers can also be unpredictable, boring, off-topic, and long-winded, so use them with care. Know how well they communicate and what they'll say before you invite them! Consider using visitors in different ways – for example have them respond to questions from members of a student panel who pose questions generated from the class.

ENCOURAGING AND HANDLING QUESTIONS

You should consider allowing students some time to raise questions with you during the lecture. However, do not be disappointed if there is no response to your Any questions? You will often need to use strategies to encourage questions, particularly early in a series of lectures when students are getting to know you. One simple method of encouraging students to think about what they are learning and to make comments or ask questions is to have them write down their comments or questions and submit these for your consideration and answer.

There are some points to remember when handling questions from students.

- Listen to the question very carefully.
- Restate the question clearly and succinctly to ensure all students have heard it. The question is.
- Consider putting the question back to the class. Does anyone have a response? Answer the question politely and precisely. Sometimes a simple yes or no will be sufficient. Avoid using the question as an excuse to give a second lecture! Our natural tendency to do so will certainly discourage questions from students in future. Be alert to the

questioner who is deliberately trying to trick or to bait you. Others may use the occasion to display their knowledge of the subject. If the questioner is particularly awkward or aggressive, handle the situation as coolly as possible. Strategies include agreeing with as much of what was said as possible, acknowledging legitimate differences of opinion or interpretation, or suggesting you meet the questioner afterwards to clarify your position. At all costs, avoid an argument in front of your class. However, do not be afraid to disagree with any questioner when you are quite sure of your ground.

STUDENT NOTE-TAKING

Much of this Guide focuses on your preparation and approaches to teaching rather than on considerations of student learning. This focus partly reflects the scope of the Guide. Nevertheless, student learning is paramount. One means of supporting learning is through student note-taking. As you deliver your lecture, be conscious of the fact that most students will wish to take some notes.

Research in the area of note-taking generally supports the view that this activity should be encouraged. It is a process that helps the student engage with the lecture and one that supports learning, especially if students revise their notes immediately after the lecture. On the other hand, research suggests that student notes are often inaccurate. If you doubt this, try the experiment of asking one or two students to loan you their notes and compare what they wrote to your own notes for the lecture. Your attention to the advice we have offered earlier about lecture preparation will assist accurate note-taking by providing clear structures for the material, and your attention to the speed of presentation, pauses, repetitions, and use of visual aids and perhaps structured handouts will also have a bearing on note-taking quality.

We suggest that you have the structure of your lecture on a slide that you display at the beginning and end of the lecture to make the structure explicit at the outset and to help revise key points at the end. Using the same slide mid-way through the lecture can help everyone to check on what has been done and where the lecture is heading.

Take time to review note-taking practices with your students and consider teaching them how to take suitable notes. Some lecturers make their notes available on the web, either in complete form, or as 'partial notes' that leave out key information, with the aim of motivating students to come to class and listen more carefully to what is being said. The book by Bligh (2000) outlines some useful ways to do this as well as the evidence for the effectiveness of the practice. If you only make the structure of your lecture explicit and take time with complex diagrams or proofs, you will have made two positive contributions to helping students with their notes.

USE OF AUDIO-VISUAL MATERIALS

The care and thought you have given to the preparation of your audio-visual materials should not be diminished by careless use of them and the equipment during the lecture. As we have stressed earlier, it is essential that you find sufficient time to practise using the audio-visual systems at a time when the lecture room is empty and available for experimentation. The following strategies on using the different media discussed in the section on preparation may prove helpful to you.

WHITEBOARDS AND CHALKBOARDS

Always start a presentation with a clean board and one that only has your material on it. Always try to avoid speaking and writing on the board at the same time. Look at the audience to facilitate hearing of what is being said. Face the board squarely and move across the board when writing. This will assist in writing horizontally.

Underline headings and important or unfamiliar words to give visual emphasis. Use dark colour pens and always carry a spare pen with you. Always avoid red and light colours for lettering which are very difficult to read from a distance. Blue and black are best for legibility.

POWERPOINT SLIDE PROJECTION

Before commencing a presentation, you should ensure that the projected image is correctly located and focused on the screen and any remote control devices are working properly. Display material for a purpose and use a 'black slide' or switch off the image as soon as the material on a slide has been dealt with to avoid having to compete with a projected image for student attention. A pointer may be a useful aid to indicate specific parts of a slide if some attention-getting device has not been built in to the presentation itself. It is now possible to buy an electronic device that combines a laser pointer with the ability to advance slides and black out the screen from any part of the room – extremely handy if you wish to move around the lecture theatre.

Pause and give students time to study each slide, and sufficient light to take notes. Most data projectors are now powerful enough for the image to be seen without dimming the lights – a change for the better, since there is nothing more sleep- inducing than a lecture in a darkened room!

Some final words of caution. The sheer mass of information some lecturers try to present using PowerPoint slides has to be seen to be believed: long lists of bullet points, slabs of text with small fonts, complex tables of raw data and graphs, and confusing and annoying use of formatting and presentation tools and university logos. Just as telling is not teaching, so showing is not teaching either!

LECTURE MANAGEMENT AND DISCIPLINE

A basic requirement for establishing good relationships between you and students and the avoidance of disciplinary problems, is to convince them that attending the lecture is worthwhile, which in turn is facilitated by lectures that are well organised, engagingly presented, and closely related to the goals of the course, including the exams and assignments. This will instil a sense of confidence in you as a teacher.

When first meeting a class, take plenty of time to introduce yourself and your lecture or lecture series. Display essential details on the whiteboard or on a well- prepared and legible slide. The first impression you make sets the tone for the class and can be lasting.

In many institutions you will have a formal obligation to explain the assessment arrangements, including a full rationale for grading practices; in other cases this can be regarded as simply good practice. Similarly, there will often be an institutional or departmental policy about student conduct in classes and you may find it useful to discuss this with students to help minimise and manage potential challenges that may arise. Some matters you may want to raise with your students include:

- your reasonable expectations for conduct in lectures and the need to keep distractions of all kinds to a minimum
- the use of mobile phones, laptops and other devices for other than teaching-related activities during class designating the last row of classroom seats (or some other area) as the available space for late arrivals and early departures.

Getting to know students will do much to prevent awkward situations arising. Breaking down anonymity barriers from the beginning of your teaching with a new group of students is a very positive step to take. If you do not meet students in tutorial or practical classes, try to arrive early at your lecture venue and depart late whenever possible so that you can get to know at least some of them and be available to offer assistance should it be requested. Deliberately getting to know those students who are challenging you in some way is a good strategy to prevent future trouble.

Biggs and Tang (2007) describe 'learning partnerships' as an initiative you might consider to help break down anonymity and to reduce the sense of isolation and alienation some students may experience. The teacher can match partners, or students can choose their own partners. Partners agree to sit together in class and consult out of class. They collaborate on class activities and prepare feedback and questions from the class as required. Students who wish to remain 'loners' should have their wish respected. Even if you do not go this far, at least make sure that students know the person sitting next to them, for example by taking three minutes early in the first class to exchange names and interests.

It is necessary to act promptly and firmly – but fairly – at early signs of disciplinary problems or unrest, first reflecting on whether your own behaviour or teaching style may be a contributing factor. Such prompt and fair action will have a positive impact on the whole class. The regular use of strategies to engage and focus students actively in the class will help to prevent these issues from arising.

You should avoid threatening comments, particularly if you have no intention of carrying them out. Threats have a negative effect on the way students perceive you as a teacher and as a person. Threats place you in the position of either having to carry them out or of losing credibility if you do not. Explaining the consequences that certain behaviours have for you and other students, waiting for silence, 'eye-balling' a recalcitrant student, and insisting that a troublemaker should leave are all strategies that might be appropriate in a given set of circumstances. If a situation is really serious, you should warn the group that you will leave unless your reasonable requirements are met. If they are not met ... then leave! Be assured that you will have the support of the majority of the group if you deal with disruptive behaviour in a fair yet firm manner. We have found that an effective strategy in many cases is simply to explain to the class what a challenging task it is to lecture to a large group of students – one that requires your full attention and which is greatly disrupted by distractions such as talking, using phones, and texting.

However, in difficult situations, do consider that a student's behaviour may be due to some factor such as difficult personal circumstances, a disability, an illness or substance abuse. Since such situations can and do arise, as a new teacher it is wise to be fully informed in advance about the services available on campus to help troubled students – such as health, counselling, and even campus security.

Although a student's behaviour may cause a temporary disruption in a lecture, this does not justify action on your part that is in any way retaliatory or vindictive in nature. At the same time, it is important to seek some quick and sound resolution of an issue with the students concerned before the next class meeting.

A most useful resource for thinking about the challenges presented by students and how lecturers have responded is the book of case studies edited by Edwards Smith and Webb (2001).

CONCLUDING THE LECTURE

Provided your time has not expired, avoid competing with a rising level of noise at the end of your lecture. If necessary, pause and insist on quiet until you reach your planned conclusion. This is the opportunity to reiterate the key points you have made earlier. Make listening to the conclusion worthwhile for students. You may also wish to direct students to additional reading. But be reasonable in your expectations and be quite specific about them. Avoid recommending a whole book if you really only need them to look at one diagram on page 99! Your closing comments will have been carefully prepared and, as they are the last words you say, are likely to be remembered best by the class.

Finally, never go over-time. Students have other commitments besides your class! If the situation suggests that an extension of time is necessary, do provide an open opportunityfor those who wish to leave to do so, but do not then penalise them by introducing new material that they have no other way of catching up on.

Chapter 4
Evaluation of Lectures

If you have some experience as a lecturer it might be advisable to start with this section and then work through the other chapters. There is an important reason for this. Research has identified something that we have all probably observed in university teaching: different lecturers, and lecturers in different disciplines have characteristic ways of lecturing, or to use the technical term, different 'styles or approaches to lecturing. For some, a reliance on oral methods seems to be common, whereas others use a variety of visual communication methods, and still others prefer problem-based group or project work. 'So what?' you may ask. Well, realistic awareness of your current style can help you determine whether you wish to strengthen aspects of that approach or whether you wish to try something different that you believe will be more effective.

Whilst experience in lecturing can be a useful teacher, it is rarely sufficient on its own. Experience is only a starting point for learning and it needs to be analysed, thought about, judged, acted upon and broadened by exposure to other possible approaches. How do we start with this process of self-evaluation, and possible change?

First, we need to consider the criteria we are using to make judgements about our teaching, then we need to act on the judgements made, and finally we need to get further feedback for subsequent evaluation.

There are several ways you can evaluate your present teaching approach and it is best if you can enlist the assistance of someone from your institution's teaching support centre to help with this process. The methods described below can be used to evaluate many characteristics of your teaching such as whether you are clearly audible, proceed too quickly, and what kind of impact you are having on students.

VIDEO RECORDING

A direct way of evaluation is to have a colleague or a member of your institution's teaching unit make a video recording of your lecture. It is advisable to have a preliminary meeting to discuss your goals for the session. When you watch the replay, it is best to do so in the company of someone who was present during the lecture. This is an important caution because you will have little appreciation of what it was like to be in the audience and your assessment of things like speed of delivery, speech, and pauses can be erroneous without the opportunity to check with someone else who was actually present in the lecture. Having a colleague watch the recording with you will also counteract the common tendency to focus more on your voice, personal appearance and mannerisms rather than on teaching strategies and student reactions.

As you watch the replay, do so against a prepared checklist of points you are particularly interested in – evidence of your preparation, eye-contact, adequacy of technical explanations, number and clarity of projected slides, management of student activities, student reaction, and so on. Use the ideas and feedback you obtain from this process in your next few lectures and then arrange a further recording to check on your progress.

A useful role for an observer is to identify what is working well and to help clarify the underlying principles of success. If necessary, an observer can also suggest concrete strategies for change, not simply give comments.

All of this is probably best done by a professional educational developer rather than a colleague. Consider how you will explain the presence of a video camera (and colleague) to your students. Remember that if students are to appear in the video they have a right to be consulted in advance.

WRITTEN RECORD OF OBSERVATIONS

A simple way of keeping a record of your lecture is to ask a colleague to sit in a lecture and keep a structured written record of what happens. Once again, it is best to have a preliminary meeting to discuss your goals for session. The observer might also find it useful to review other course materials, such as the course syllabus, handouts, and assignments. These activities can lead to a fully-fledged peer consultation process in which colleagues work together over time to observe each other's teaching, suggest possible strategies for change, and monitor the effectiveness of such changes on students' learning. For a more comprehensive guide to peer consultation and evaluation see Knapper and Piccinin (1999).

This record kept of the lecture forms the basis for subsequent discussion and analysis. We find that the following series of headings across the top of a sheet of paper provides a useful structure.

Time:	Lecturer activity:	Student activity:	Comments:

As a lecture proceeds, a record of time is kept against descriptions of what you and your students are doing at that time, together with evaluative comments or suggestions for subsequent discussion.

QUESTIONNAIRES

Nearly all universities and colleges use student questionnaires administered at the end of term to evaluate courses and lecturers. Use of these instruments is often controversial, but despite possible methodical flaws they undoubtedly do provide useful feedback about students' perceptions of teaching. Unfortunately such feedback usually comes too late to make changes – except for the next time the course is offered. Another problem with such evaluations is that they usually offer rather blanket judgements (this teacher was good, poor, very poor) and rarely provide much in the way of constructive suggestions for change. Because of these shortcomings many lecturers decide to construct and administer their own questionnaires for use at an earlier point in a course of lectures, where the feedback can serve as a basis for possible changes. Such questionnaires can be tailored to the particular needs of the course, instructor, and context and your teaching and learning centre will almost certainly be able to help you design an instrument. There are also many relevant resources available on the web. For example, the two sites: https://www.queensu.ca/registrar/usat/invent.html and http://www.adelaide.edu.au/clpd/selt/ list many possible questions on different aspects of teaching, grouped by category. Standard lecture questionnaires are widely available, and your institution's teaching and learning centre should be able to supply you with one to use and help you in interpreting the results. Try it out and be prepared to act on the information it yields.

A questionnaire need not be long to get useful information. In fact just asking three or four focussed questions towards the end of class can yield extremely useful information. This was the impetus behind the concept of 'classroom assessment techniques' popularised in the USA by Angelo and Cross (1993) as a means of gathering information from students as a regular part of effective teaching. The idea is quite simple: at a suitable break in the lecture the teacher poses three or four questions that relate to the teaching, the material being taught, or any other aspect of learning that is thought to be of concern. For example, students might be asked:

• What did you like best about today's class, so far?
• What did you like least?
• What changes would you suggest that would help improve your learning?

Alternatively, the questions could focus on lecture content, such as:

• What was the most important thing you learned in the class today?
• What concepts or ideas do you feel you do not fully understand?
• What could the lecturer do to help your understanding?

The possibilities are endless, and each set of questions is best devised by the lecturer to suit his or her needs – though Angelo and Cross give numerous examples. Note that the questions we have provided in the examples are open-ended, which generally provide fuller information than closed-ended items, though these can also be used. There is no need to have the questionnaires printed in advance – they can simply be shown on a PowerPoint slide or an overhead transparency. Students respond by tearing a page from their notebook and are asked to drop their questionnaires in a box on leaving the lecture. You might also suggest that, in addition to answering the lecturer's questions, if they have any additional comments, concerns or questions about the course so far they are welcome to add them.

The whole process need not take long, and in fact, another name for this technique is the 'minute paper' and this is described in Angelo and Cross.

One important point to make about this type of exercise, whether of the short form or a longer more formal mid-term questionnaire, is that you should introduce it by explaining to students why you are asking for this information and what you will do with the results. At the following class, after you have analysed the feedback you should provide students with a short summary and say what possible changes you will make as a result. This is a very tangible way of convincing students you are concerned about their needs and their learning.

DISCUSSIONS WITH STUDENTS

Gathering information about teaching can be used to good effect in your attempts to understand the processes of student learning. Students will often give you useful insights into such things as their methods of note-taking, their concepts of issues and topics in the course, and the relative amounts of assigned and independent work they do. If you proceed sensitively, students need not feel threatened by your questioning of their academic work and their reactions to it. Simply arriving early and departing late from a class will give you opportunities to talk to students.

As well as gathering feedback in these ways, you can consult students in a more systematic way, for example by using the peer consultant approach mentioned earlier. Here, your colleague not only observes your teaching but can also meet with a sample of students to explore their perceptions and gather their suggestions in a non-threatening setting. Some lecturers even appoint a 'student advisory committee' to offer comments and suggestions throughout the course.

ACTING ON EVALUATIVE DATA

A reasonably comprehensive evaluation of your lecturing should give you reliable insights into each of the characteristics of the effective teacher discussed in Chapter 1 The Effective Lecturer. These characteristics, remember, were: organisation, instruction, evaluation and feedback, relationships, engagement, and subject knowledge. Student evaluation is not a reliable indicator of subject knowledge, which is better assessed by a peer.

Having information and insights is, of course, only one step to improving your teaching approach. Assuming you have the will to do something about what you have learned of your lecturing, how can you change? Apart from enrolling in a course that addresses postsecondary teaching and student learning, you can embark on either a program of self-help and reading or, better still, work with a trusted colleague towards your goals.

This Guide is designed to assist you in both courses of action. Working alone has advantages of privacy but rules out the possibility of fresh ideas and the support and encouragement a trusted colleague or a member of the staff of a teaching unit can offer. If you are working alone, try to select one particular attribute or a group of attributes for attention at any one time. For example, if you are proceeding too quickly for most of the class, you might consider giving some thought to the following:

- The structure of the lecture, and how you explain that structure to students (perhaps students are getting lost during the lecture)
- The beginning of the lecture (perhaps students do not have a clear idea of where you are heading)
- Use of variations and activities to provide breaks to enhance concentration and to help with student understanding)
- Use of visual aids (too much information on slides? enough time to study information on slides?)
- Speaking too quickly and not clearly.

Rarely are teaching difficulties attributable to one source alone. There are usually several factors operating as the above example shows. And there are the complicating factors of departmental politics, personalities, and relationships that are beyond the scope of this Guide and which may require professional help over the longer term.

Chapter 5
Moving From Teacher Telling to Student Learning In Lectures

The first part of this Guide has described some fundamental techniques of lecturing. It concentrated on ways of preparing and presenting lectures. But the quotation at the beginning of this Guide warns us that 'telling' is not necessarily the same as teaching. Unfortunately it is common to find lecturers adopting telling behaviours such as repeating material from textbooks or other sources readily available to students, and in some extreme cases, actually reading the textbook, word-for-word, to students!

The defence for doing these sorts of things in lectures rests on the claim that we need to transfer information to students to provide a basis for future learning and future teaching. But there are major limitations of telling to facilitate transfer and promote learning. First, telling someone something does not automatically – or even usually – mean that it is understood. Second, there is a margin for serious error in the transfer process from the original source—lecturer's preparation—lecturer's presentation—student notes—student understanding. The evidence suggests students will only note a fraction of the material the lecturer regards as very important and, even if they have listened carefully, one must ask how much will be either recalled or understood. Bligh (2000) is one source that provides salutary insights into this issue.

Research discussed earlier in this Guide suggests that learning, especially the sort of deep learning needed for critical thinking and problem-solving, is achieved much more readily when students are actively engaged in some kind of meaningful task. Even if it is true that lectures can provide a basis of common information on which students can build, the 'telling and transfer' model of teaching is certainly over- used in higher education. The question we must ask ourselves as we plan teaching is how much of 'the basics' are required before students can be trusted to learn independently, which is something that nearly all academics wish to encourage.

It is a great irony that lecturing is still so common in universities, some 500 years after the invention of the printing press and the more recent web-based technologies for making information so freely available to students.

However, there is still a place for presenting information, ideas and insights through lectures, for example when information is not readily available to students from any other source. The preceding chapters have shown how such presentations can be made more effective by careful preparation and structuring, appropriate use of educational technologies, and the use of variety. These strategies will lead you away from the danger of engaging in simple 'telling' behaviours. So, if you wish to actually teach rather than tell, and to help students to learn, what else can you do?

This partly depends on the goals of your course. Earlier, we suggested that lectures might have a number of worthwhile learning goals other than presenting information about a subject. These purposes include the encouragement of deeper learning, such as developing conceptual understanding, thinking and problem - solving skills, and in particular the ability to apply what has been learned in new situations.

If these are the goals, then the basic principle to keep in mind is that students must be placed in a situation where they do more than listen and are challenged to think for themselves and actually engage in solving problems. Lectures may not be the ideal setting in which to achieve this, but with a little thought and planning they can help with the process. Two rather different strategies for achieving such goals are outlined below

QUESTIONING TECHNIQUES

Questioning is an important teaching skill and one that is frequently neglected in higher education. Questioning has intellectual, motivational and disciplinary purposes. Its intellectual purposes include stimulating recall and encouraging thinking and reasoning. The motivational and disciplinary purposes are, in a sense, linked: questions can be used to generate interest, and direct wandering attention to the task you have set.
Skill in basic questioning technique is essential before you can develop competence in the more advanced questioning skills outlined below.

BASIC QUESTIONING TECHNIQUE

- Ask the question. Be clear and concise, ensure all can hear you. Try to begin with words such as 'how', 'what', 'why', 'when', 'which', 'give an example of' When phrasing your question, try to avoid questions that lead to right or wrong answers, which some students will see as threatening and therefore resist answering. Rather, ask more open-ended questions which are less threatening and may lead to further discussion. Pause. Allow each student time to think.
- Name the student or group who is to give the answer (always name after a question is asked to encourage thinking among all students and not just the one named). A copy of the class roll can be a helpful guide to distributing questions fairly among the class.
- Listen to the answer given. Evaluate the answer, and perhaps repeat it. Some kind of feedback is crucial. Probe (optional). If necessary challenge the student to elaborate or to clarify the response.
- Redirect (optional). If the first student cannot answer, redirect the question to another. Avoid the temptation to immediately answer yourself.
- Close. Link student response with teaching, and continue.

ADVANCED QUESTIONING: QUESTIONS TO STIMULATE THINKING

Advanced questioning does not refer to a more complex question-asking procedure. It refers to raising the intellectual level at which students are challenged to think and to respond. Studies of higher education classes show that the majority of questions asked by teachers are at the lowest cognitive levels and that this is true even in advanced-level courses. It follows that students are receiving little practice in applying higher-order cognitive processes during their classes, which in many courses accounts for the greater part of the student's contact time with the subject.

Let us look at some lower and higher-level questions to see what might be done.

- Lower cognitive level: recall-type questions ask students to state facts, definitions, relationships or procedures previously learned. Examples:
- Who is the Prime Minister of Canada ?
- Name three techniques for stimulating thinking in lectures.

- Higher cognitive level: a variety of levels you might find appropriate are as follows:
  (i) Understanding, translation, interpretation. These questions require students to go beyond that which is given to demonstrate their comprehension or ability to translate, interpret, and/or infer.
  Examples:
    - What are the main issues addressed by the author?
    - Express that idea in your own words.
    - From this evidence, what conclusions could we draw?
    - Give another example of the concept we have been discussing.

- (ii) Evaluation. Evaluative questions demand some form of judgement against criteria.
  Examples:
    - What errors were made in the research design?(and what criteria did you use?)
    - How adequate is that proposal? (and, what criteria did you use?)
    - How accurate is that answer? (and, what standard did you apply?)

- (iii) Problem-solving. This group is broad indeed. It includes analysis questions (which require the breaking-down of something into parts), synthesis questions (which require putting ideas together or creating a new idea) and application questions (which require the recall of ideas or information for use in novel situations).
  Examples:
    - How could we satisfactorily explain that lecturer's reaction? (analysis)
    - Formulate an hypothesis that could be tested for this problem. (synthesis)
    - What theorem would be appropriate here? Why? (application)

When questioning at the higher cognitive levels it needs to be remembered that questions will not function at the higher level if students can simply recall the data, problem, situation, or issue referred to by the question. Novelty is essential if the question is to stimulate higher-level thinking and not simply prompt recall or recognition-type responses.

In all questioning, the purpose must be constructive and directed towards understanding. Questioning can easily become threatening and destructive in the hands of an insensitive teacher and this will certainly cause many students to 'disengage' with your classes and possibly not turn up at all. Better ways of asking and encouraging questions include:

- Ask questions in ways that elicit responses that reflect student's own experiences
- Early in your teaching, avoiding right-wrong type questions which may embarrass students is a strategy to help boost their confidence and develop their trust in you
- For similar reasons, ask questions without a single correct answer
- Direct questions to pairs or groups rather than to individuals
- Allow time for the development of responses, including having students write answers and submit these for consideration
- Don't respond to answers prematurely
- Distribute questions and tasks around the class and do not let a few individuals dominate the answering
- Provide feedback, clarification, praise and correction where necessary
- Physically move around the classroom during a question period.

ACTIVE LEARNING SESSIONS

Throughout this Guide we have repeated the idea (hopefully to the point of redundancy) that variation in the lecture is desirable and that one form of variation is to provide a break from listening to long periods of discourse – the 'tyranny of telling'! Time for active learning where thinking, discussion or problem-solving is required can be most useful for both you and your students. Some examples of activities are given below. The time required for the activity must be carefully thought through: it needs to be adequate for the majority of students to complete not so short that it becomes a speed-exercise that no-one completes, nor so long that lecture time is wasted in idle conversation. The activity must be planned not as an end in itself – as a simple, short rest break might be – but as an activity designed to help students understand the material or to assess their understanding.

There is ample evidence that introducing activities into lectures, when done appropriately, is valued by students (for example, Machemer & Crawford, 2007) and is indeed effective in encouraging engagement – and hence facilitating attention, comprehension, and learning. One very simple study showed an increase in student engagement in lectures by implementing small-scale activities at 20, 30 and 40 minutes after commencing a lecture. These activities were asking students to write down what they had learned, writing down one question they would like answered, and taking a short break (Dyson, 2008). This study illustrates a much wider consensus that supports the idea that student-centred approaches in teaching will increase student engagement and learning (Biggs & Tang, 2007; Ramsden, 2003).

Active learning sessions and breaks can be of two main kinds; those activities designed to engage individual students and those designed to encourage students to interact with each other. Here are a few examples of activities, presented from the simple to more complex. Example 1: Answering a multiple-choice question A question, perhaps in a multiple-choice format, can be displayed on an overhead transparency or PowerPoint slide for all to answer. Asking for a show of hands for each alternative can enable you to check understanding. Modern student response systems, including using mobile telephones and 'clickers' may be available in your institution to assist you and you should direct enquiries to the appropriate support services about this. (For recent discussion of the application of clickers, go to the Annual Conference Proceedings on the HERDSA website http://www.herdsa.org.au/ and search under 'clickers'.)

Follow up by explaining why each alternative is or is not a suitable answer, or even better, encourage students with different answers to argue for their choice and encourage others to provide feedback.

Suggested Minimum Time Required:
    For question working - 2 minutes
    Follow-up and discussion - 5 minutes
    Total - about 7 minutes

Example 2: Think-Pair-Share

Think-Pair-Share is a strategy to engage students in actively thinking about an issue or problem in classes of any size. After asking a carefully prepared question, tell students to think silently about their answers and allow a reasonable time for this. Then ask students to pair up with another to compare or discuss their responses. You may then call randomly on a few pairs to summarize their discussion or give their answer. The random calls are a way to communicate your expectation that all students are to participate in these kinds of activities.

Suggested Minimum Time Required:
    For individual question working - 2 minutes
    Pair discussion – 3 minutes
    Follow-up and class discussion - 5 minutes
    Total - about 10 minutes

A more developed version of think-pair-share is given below:

Example 3: Reading (or problem-solving) and discussion Many variations of this strategy are possible and it can be set up as either an individual task or as something for pairs of students or small groups to work on. One example is described. Students are instructed to bring their text to lectures or a handout is distributed with, perhaps, an abstract of an article, a quotation, a summary, a set of diagrams, photographs, or equations, or a simple and legible statement is projected for all to study.

A directed reading or interpretation task, or problem is set related to what you have been discussing in the lecture. This task should involve students for no more than 5-10 minutes. At the conclusion of the task, students are instructed to do something: for example, to compare answers, draw conclusions, raise issues, identify misunderstandings, or to make evaluative judgements with the person seated beside them. Feedback is then asked for. Depending on the size of the group you could ask for reports from all or some of the pairs, have pairs report to another pair and seek general reports from these larger groups, have a show of hands to questions or issues you have identified as you moved around the class during the discussion phase, or have students write on cards, collect these, deal with points made in the lecture or collate the information after the lecture as a basis for your teaching in the next lecture.

Conclude by drawing ideas together, summing up, or whatever is appropriate to the task. Whatever you do – and this is particularly critical in larger groups – thoroughly plan the activity: clearly structure the time and the tasks set, and stick to your plan (unless there are very good reasons to change). Your instructions, including the time available and tasks to be carried out, should be clearly displayed on a handout, a transparency or on the board for ready reference during the exercise.

Suggested Minimum Time Required:
    Instructions and explanation - 3 minutes
    Reading/problem-solving - 5-10 minutes
    Paired discussion - 5 minutes
    Feedback session - 10 minutes
    Conclusion, summing up - 5 minutes
    Total - about 30 minutes

Example 4: Pro-and-Con Grid and discussion
A useful active learning strategy, and a strategy for helping you to assess student understanding, is the Pro-and-Con Grid (Angelo & Cross, 1993). The grid provides a quick overview of a class's analysis of an issue of concern and forces students to go beyond their first reactions to search for different perspectives and to weigh the value of competing claims. If the results of the activity are submitted at the end of a lecture, the

student's responses will give an appreciation of the depth and breadth of their analyses. Alternatively, the results of individual students' work, and that of pairs or small groups can form the basis of a brief discussion.

Students are asked, individually, in pairs or small groups of 3 or 4, to identify the pros and cons on a grid in relation to a judgement, dilemma, proposition, strategy or issue. After a short period of work, the results are then discussed and outcomes related back to the subject of the lecture.

Suggested Minimum Time Required:
    Instructions and explanation - 2 minutes
    Individual/pair/group work - 5 minutes
    Feedback session - 10 minutes
    Conclusion, summing up - 3 minutes
    Total - about 20 minutes

As you move into the use of discussion techniques to engage students, you will need to be confident in the techniques you intend to use. The HERDSA Guide Conducting Tutorials (2009) by Lublin and Sutherland is recommended as a reference to support you in this work.

RESOURCES FOR OTHER ACTIVE LEARNING STRATEGIES IN LECTURES

Many resources are available to supplement the ideas presented in this Guide. Some of the strategies they describe are relatively simple and are easy to use. Others are more complex. In all cases, careful preparation is required of both the task and the time for the activity.

As well as providing the necessary activity for students to help them develop their understanding of the subject, many activities provide you with valuable and direct feedback on their learning and, indirectly, on your teaching. Equally important is monitoring an activity as it proceeds and being ready to provide assistance to students so that they can participate effectively in your active learning lecture.

The following resources will provide you with further examples for active learning.

ACTIVE LEARNING IN HIGHER EDUCATION

This journal is a particularly rich source of current research papers and practical ideas for engaging students in worthwhile learning activities in lectures.
Angelo, T. & Cross, K. P. (1993). Classroom assessment techniques: A handbook for college teachers (2nd ed.). San Francisco: Jossey-Bass.

This book is particularly helpful in that it describes active learning strategies that also give you feedback on student understanding of what you are teaching them. We strongly recommend this book to you.

Astin, A. W. (1999). Student involvement: A developmental theory for higher education. Journal of College Student Development, 40, 518-529.
This article is a straightforward introduction to the ideas of active involvement and engagement of students in higher education. Those who wish to explore the idea further should consult the index of Pascarella and Terenzini (2005). An excellent, up-to-date review can also be found on Wikipedia under the heading of 'student engagement'.

Bean, J. C. (1996). Engaging ideas: The professor's guide to integrating writing critical thinking, and active learning in the classroom. San Francisco: Jossey-Bass.(A revised edition is to be published in 2011.)

The title summarises what this book is about; it shows how writing can be integrated with active learning strategies including interactive lectures.

Bligh, D. A. (2000). What's the use of lectures? San Francisco: Jossey-Bass.

This classic on lecturing is very well worth reading even though some of the material is now dated. Possibly still the most comprehensive and thorough discussion of lecturing and of ways to improve practice. Original edition published by Penguin (1972) and later edition published by Intellect (2006).

Pascarella, E. T. & Terenzini, P. T. (2005). How college affects students: A third decade of research. San Francisco: Jossey-Bass.

This is an outstanding review of research on higher education rather than a book of strategies for teaching. It is included here as an important resource for readers who wish to add depth to their understanding of the evidence for the importance of student-teacher engagement and active learning. Summaries provided are especially helpful. See also Astin, above.

Although there are numerous books available on lecturing, initially it may be much easier to simply Google 'lectures', 'lecturing technique' or 'large group teaching' If this does not yield more than enough samples for you, try one or more of these resources to get you started for specific, discipline-based, examples of what lecturers have done to improve the quality of their teaching. The teaching and learning centre at your and many other universities will also have a comprehensive set of resources online.

Material and research on lecturing developed in New Zealand and Australia can be found by searching conference proceedings and other materials on the HERDSA website: http://www.herdsa.org.au

Canadian examples of lectures and large group teaching can be accessed through the Society for Teaching and Learning in Higher Education (STLHE) website: http://www.stlhe.ca
Finally, the Australian Teaching Large Classes Project website has a useful range of resources: http://www.tedi.uq.edu.au/largeclasses

Relationships between lectures and other methods

The relationships between your lectures and the other teaching methods used in your academic department may vary from almost non-existent, through strong relationships, to overlapping. What does this mean?

First, there is an important administrative relationship to consider. In some courses the timetabling and staffing problems are advanced as reasons why the lectures, tutorials, and practical classes are not closely co-ordinated. This is a serious problem where tutorials and labs are intended to reinforce lecture material. The solutions to this problem seem to lie in administrative action but you should keep the problem in mind as you teach and consciously make as many links between the different parts of the course as you can.

Second, there is the conceptual relationship. A strong conceptual relationship exists where the lectures, tutorials, labs and assignments closely support one another. The closer they are together in time and in content, the stronger the relationship will be. In some universities and colleges successful experiments have been made with longer teaching periods to strengthen this relationship and to simplify course administration. In one case a two-hour period was divided as follows:

- 30 minutes: introductory lecture/organisation (course TAs in attendance)
- 60 minutes: small group tutorials (involving all TAs assigned to the course and the lecturer)
- 30 minutes: concluding plenary/lecture (including group reports, questions, summary).

The general principle of dividing time in this way can also be applied in the traditional 50-minute lecture. An example was suggested above where reading, discussion, or problem-solving might occur. It will be objected that there is just not time for this kind of activity. This objection rests on the argument that material has to be 'covered' but in our view the argument is misguided and mistaken in confusing 'seat time' and 'coverage' with learning: the silly notion that just because the lecturer has said something, it has been attended to by students and understood. The task of the teacher is not to 'cover' something but to uncover through explanation and clarification that helps students to understand.

Evidence shows that levels of attention to the traditional expository lecture, and other indicators of performance – such as recall and even pulse rates – decline fairly rapidly starting from about 20 minutes after the lecture begins. Worse, what little is learned in the remainder of the lecture interferes with understanding of earlier material. The coverage argument also wrongly assumes that lectures are the only way of providing material to students – as if printing presses and the web had yet to be invented. So perhaps the question you should be asking yourself is, Should I be wasting time speaking for 50 minutes?

The problem of student learning is unfortunately much greater than this. It is the case that not all students regard lectures as an important learning activity at all. At best, it seems, lectures are perceived as being a means to pace study, as a way of keeping in touch with the course work, and as supplementary to other more important learning activities. At worst, lectures are seen as a boring waste of time relieved only by the skill and daring of the paper plane throwers and other attention seekers!

A challenge to teachers in higher education is to work out clear and educationally defensible strategies for lecturing that help students to learn. And, as we observed before, well-thought out lectures can be a useful learning method for students. It can also be a personally rewarding and interesting task for academic staff. It is hoped that this Guide will contribute to dealing with these challenges and possibilities.

Chapter 6
Recommended Reading

Several recommendations for further reading have been placed throughout the text. We suggest the following additional titles as the basis for a reading program to enhance your understanding of teaching in higher education with particular reference to lectures and large group teaching:

Andrews, R. (2010). *Argumentation in higher education: Improving practice through theory and research.* London: Routledge.

This book is suggested once you feel comfortable with your lecturing and wish to develop your teaching strategies around the idea of improving students' abilities in argument in your discipline. Not suggested for the novice.

Biggs, J. & Tang, C. (2007). *Teaching for quality learning at university: What the student does (3rd ed.). Maidenhead*, Berkshire: Society for Research into Higher Education and Open University Press.

This is an outstanding book of practical theory and straightforward advice on teaching and learning in universities that includes a chapter of specific relevance to this Guide: 'Enriching large-class teaching'. Useful for those who are seeking sound, evidence-based, ideas to move beyond lecturing.

Brown, S. & Race, P. (2002). *Lecturing, a practical guide.* London: Kogan Page.

For teachers seeking guidance on practical exercises they might carry out to improve their lecturing, this book has few peers. The book is divided into units that look at explaining, lecturing and student notes. The units contain 45 different activities that can be carried out individually or in groups.

Cannon, R. & Newble, D. (2000). *A handbook for teachers in universities and colleges* (4th ed.). London: Kogan Page.

Chapters on teaching large classes and making conference presentations extend the material presented in this Guide. However, the book is especially helpful for those wishing to take the first steps in a reading program as it helpfully introduces a wide range of related teaching concerns such as curriculum planning and assessment. The chapters on student learning and student-centred learning support these two concepts introduced in this Guide.

Edwards, H., Smith, B. & Webb, G. (2001). *Lecturing: Case studies, experience and practice.* London: Kogan Page.

This book will appeal to all lecturers who seeking ways to understand and improve their practice. The case studies give rich, real-life insights into the actual experience of lecturing from a broad range of disciplines in different countries.

Gibbs, G. & Jenkins, A. (Eds.). (1992). *Teaching large classes in higher education: How to maintain quality with reduced resources.* London: Kogan Page.

This collection of essays includes case study accounts of ways university teachers are managing very large classes. It goes well beyond exemplars of lecture-type teaching and discusses other teaching approaches and related matters such as fieldwork, assessment, and ways in which institutions can support their teaching staff.

Race, P. (2007). *The Lecturer's tool kit: A practical guide to assessment, learning and teaching* (3rd ed.). London: Routledge.

This book addresses practical strategies for lecturing but that also goes further into the important and related areas of learning, assessment and other approaches to learning and teaching including on line learning and small groups.

References

Andrews, R. (2010). *Argumentation in higher education: Improving practice through theory and research.* London: Routledge.

Angelo, T. & Cross, K. P. (1993). *Classroom assessment techniques: A handbook for college teachers* (2nd ed.). San Francisco: Jossey-Bass.

Astin, A. W. (1999). Student involvement: A developmental theory for higher education. *Journal of College Student Development*, 40, 518-529.

Bailey, R. & Garner, M. (2010). Is the feedback in higher education assessment worth the paper it is written on? Teachers' reflections on their practices. *Teaching in Higher Education,* 15, 187-198.

Berk. R. A. (1996). Student ratings of 10 strategies for using humor in college teaching. *Journal on Excellence in College Teaching*, 7(3), 71-92.

Biggs, J. & Tang, C. (2007). *Teaching for quality learning at university: What the student does* (3rd ed.). Maidenhead, Berkshire: Society for Research into Higher Education and Open University Press.

Bligh, D. A. (2000). *What's the Use of Lectures?* San Francisco: Jossey-Bass.

Carini, R. M., Kuh, G. D. & Klein, S. P. (2006). Student engagement and student learning: testing the linkages. *Research in Higher Education,* 47, 1-32.

Cathcart, T. & Klein, D. (2007). *Plato and a platypus walk into a bar Understanding philosophy through jokes.* New York: Penguin.

Dyson, B. J. (2008). Assessing small-scale interventions in large-scale teaching. *Active Learning in Higher Education,* 9, 265-282.

Edwards, H., Smith, B. & Webb, G. (2001). *Lecturing: Case studies, experience and practice.* London: Kogan Page.

Faraday, M. (1960). Advice to a lecturer. London: The *Royal Institution*.

Grootenboer, P. (2010). Affective development in university education. *Higher Education Research and Development*, 29, 723-737.

Hattie, J. & Timperley, H. (2007). The power of feedback. *Review of Educational Research, 77,* 81-112.

Hogan, D. &Kwiatkowski, R. (1998). Emotional aspects of large group teaching. *Human Relations,* 51, 1403-1417.

Kennedy, N. F., Senses, N. & Ayan, P. (2011). Grasping the social through movies. *Teaching in Higher Education,* 16, 1-14.

Knapper, C. K. & Cropley, A. (2000). *Lifelong learning in higher education* (3rd.). London: Kogan Page.

Knapper, C. K. & Piccinin, S. (Eds.). (1999). *Using consultants to improve teaching. New directions for teaching and learning,* No. 79. San Francisco: Jossey Bass.

Linke R. D. & Venz, M. I. (1978). *Understanding and misconceptions in physical science.* Adelaide: Educational Research Unit, The Flinders University of South Australia.

Lublin, J. & Sutherland, K. A. (2009). Conducting tutorials (2nd ed.). Milperra, *NSW: Higher Education Research & Development Society of Australasia* (HERDSA).

Machemer, P. L. & Crawford, P. (2007). Student perceptions of active learning in a large cross-disciplinary classroom. *Active Learning in Higher Education*, 8, 9-30.

Mager, R. F. (1968). *Developing attitude toward learning.* Palo Alto, CA: Fearon.

Murray, H. G. (1991). Effective teaching behaviors in the college classroom. In J. Smart (Ed.), Higher education: *Handbook of theory and research. Volume 7.* New York: Agathon.

McCroskey, J.C. (1968). *An introduction to rhetorical communication.* Englewood Cliffs, NJ: Prentice-Hall.

Mulryan-Kyne, C. (2010). Teaching large classes at college and university level: Challenges and opportunities. Teaching in Higher Education, 15, 175-185.

Pascarella, E. T. & Terenzini, P. T. (2005). *How college affects students: A third decade of research.* San Francisco: Jossey-Bass.

Powell, J. P., and Andresen, L. W. (1985). Humour and teaching in higher education. *Studies in Higher Education,* 10, 79-90.

Ramsden, P. (2003). *Learning to teach in higher education* (2nd ed.). London: Routledge Falmer.

Spence, R. B. (1928). Lecture and class discussion in teaching educational psychology. *Journal of Educational Psychology*, 19, 454-462.

Taras, M. (2010). Student self-assessment: Processes and consequences. *Teaching in Higher Education*, 15, 199-209.

Tufte, E. (2006). *Beautiful evidence*. Cheshire, CT: Graphics Press.

About STLHE

A MESSAGE FROM ARSHAD AHMAD, PRESIDENT

Thank you for your interest in STLHE's Green Guides Series, which are one of its signature publications. STLHE members enjoy numerous benefits including its annual conference, an online networking guide and access to its international STLHE Listserv. Members also receive a bi-annual Newsletter, The Canadian Journal on the Scholarship of Teaching & Learning, Collected Essays on Learning and Teaching and occasionally books published by its members.

Founded in 1981, STLHE is a diverse and vibrant community of educators, including college and university faculty, educational developers, administrators, national award winning teachers, special interest groups and students. There is deep expertise within STLHE, and a shared commitment to advocate for good practice in teaching and learning in higher education.

STLHE has two primary constituencies served by executives of the Educational Developers Caucus, the Council of 3M National Teaching Fellows and is home to several Special Interest Groups. It's organizational structure, and Incorporation documents provide important information about its constitution, bylaws and governance.

Please visit our website at www.stlhe.ca.

OUR VISION & STRATEGY

STLHE strives to be the pre-eminent national voice, and a world leader, for enhancing teaching and learning in higher education. STLHE supports research, its dissemination, increased awareness, and application of research through scholarly teaching and learning.

We are very excited to officially announce the creation of Teaching and Learning Canada/ Apprentissage Médiation Enseignement Canada (TLC/AME)*, a charitable arm of the Society where your donation is tax-deductible. TLC aim's to leverage several of our activities and events by exploring and disseminating some of the major questions in post-secondary education.

OUR GOALS

The STLHE vision and strategy are enabled by a number of goals articulated below:
– to support and advance teaching and learning in higher education
– to provide a forum for the exchange of ideas and networking opportunities

- to provide opportunities for professional development
- to facilitate and disseminate research on teaching and learning
- to recognize and reward contributions to teaching excellence, educational leadership, innovation, service and mentorship in higher education
- to collaborate with like-minded teacher and student groups and organizations in Canada and abroad
- to shape, influence and lead policy decisions that enhance teaching and learning in higher education at local, national and international levels
- to carry out the work of the Society in Canada's two official languages – to extend the work of the Society through the creation of Teaching and Learning Canada, a charitable foundation
- to actively engage student participation in all aspects of the Society's work

BOARD OF DIRECTORS

The Board of Directors has recently proposed to elect its members on the basis of portfolio expertise to oversee the Society's activities. They meet twice a year at STLHE Conferences and each month on line.

The Board's proposal will elect Chairs to champion Bilingual, Student and College Advocacy, as well as to oversee Publications, Partnerships, Awards and Teaching and Learning Canada. An Assistant will support its Administrator works with members, the Treasurer, Secretary, Vice-President and the President.

While STLHE has a "working Board", there are numerous volunteer efforts of enthusiastic Society members also take on leadership roles in organizing the Society's activities.

JOIN US!

If you are interested in a forum for exchange of ideas and information on post-secondary teaching and learning, if you believe that teaching is important and that dedication to its improvement should be recognized, if you feel that the road to professional improvement is best walked in the company of enthusiastic peers, and if you wish to improve the quality of teaching for our students, then please join STLHE.

Your membership will strengthen the aims of the Society and will give you a chance to meet like-minded colleagues who deeply care about learning and teaching.

For more information on individual and institutional membership, please visit the Society's website www.stlhe.ca or www.sapes.ca

Arshad Ahmad
President, STLHE
3M National Teaching Fellow
email: president@stlhe.ca

Ordering Green Guides

To order please contact:

The Bookstore at Western
University Community Centre
The University of Western Ontario
London, ON N6A 3K7
Canada

Tel: (519) 661-3520
Fax: (519) 661-3673
Email: bkstor@uwo.ca
Web: www.bookstore.uwo.ca